Disasters

Learning the lessons for a safer world

David Eves

Published 2010

© David Eves 2010
Printed in England by the Lavenham Press Limited

ISBN 978 0 901357 46 5

Published by IOSH Services Ltd
The Grange
Highfield Drive
Wigston
Leicestershire
LE18 1NN
UK
t +44 (0)116 257 3100
f +44 (0)116 257 3101
www.iosh.co.uk

Mixed Sources
Product group from well-managed forests and other controlled sources
www.fsc.org Cert no. SGS-COC-004865
© 1996 Forest Stewardship Council
FSC

Contents

Dedication

To my dear wife, whose infinite patience and constant support have allowed me to write this book.

Preface

No man is an Island, entire of itself; every man is a piece of the Continent, part of the main; if a clod be washed away by the sea, Europe is the less, as well as if a promontory were, as well as if a Manor of thy friends or of thine own were; any man's death diminishes me, because I am involved in Mankind; and therefore never send to know for whom the bell tolls; It tolls for thee.

From *Devotions upon emergent occasions*, number 17, written in 1624 by John Donne, poet and Dean of St Paul's Cathedral

Acknowledgments

I am deeply indebted to the many friends and colleagues who have allowed me to pick their brains, to the vast stores of information contained on departmental, agency and encyclopaedic websites, to the authors of far more erudite books about disasters, such as Professors Brian Toft and Trevor Kletz, whose work has inspired me to have a go myself, and to Alex Cameron of IOSH for his invaluable editorial help.

About the author

David Eves CB has worked in occupational safety and health since 1964, when he joined Her Majesty's Factory Inspectorate. Formerly Deputy Director General of the Health and Safety Executive and HM Chief Inspector of Factories, he has been an Honorary Vice-President of IOSH since 1992. He is currently Vice-President of Safety Groups UK, an Ambassador for the National Examination Board for Occupational Safety and Health, and External Examiner for the Postgraduate Diploma in Regulatory Occupational Health and Safety at the University of Warwick's School of Law.

David has also conducted regulatory reviews of animal health and welfare for DEFRA. He is a member of the Royal Society for the Prevention of Accidents' National Occupational Safety and Health Committee and the Chartered Institute of Environmental Health's Policy Development Board. In 2009 he was made an Honorary Fellow of the International Institute of Safety and Risk Management.

He is co-author with the Rt Hon John Gummer MP of *Questioning performance: the director's essential guide to health, safety and the environment* (published by IOSH in 2005, revised and reprinted 2007, 2008 and 2009).

Introduction

Someone has paid the 'tuition fees'. There is no need for you to pay them again.
(Professor Trevor Kletz)

Disasters always hit the headlines. The ability of global television news to bring scenes of devastation directly into our homes enables us all to shudder and point the finger of blame, and when an industrial or public safety disaster occurs and a major company is involved, trial by the media has often taken place long before a court of inquiry begins deciding what went wrong. Corporate and individual reputations will be tarnished, sometimes damaged beyond repair.

Every inquiry into a major catastrophe demands that 'lessons should be learned'. Too often these are soon forgotten, the same mistakes repeated later. Some disasters we ought never to forget because they point the way towards a safer world, for which many people have paid a price with their lives.

In today's global economy, companies large and small are operating across continents, in diverse cultures and regulatory regimes. Society everywhere now expects governments to demand that companies avoid killing or injuring people or harming the environment. When things go very badly wrong, they want directors called to account; if gross negligence is discovered, serious consequences must follow. Witness, for example, the political response to some recent disasters in the UK – the Corporate Manslaughter and Corporate Homicide Act 2007.

My aim in writing *Disasters: learning the lessons for a safer world* was not to be censorious. That can safely be left to judges, the media and the supreme court of public opinion. My hope is that this collection of short stories will reinforce our collective memory of hard-earned lessons and help someone, somewhere, avoid another catastrophe. There are successes as well as failures to discuss and telling stories seems a good way of passing on knowledge and understanding why things can go so badly wrong.

When it came to deciding what to include, there was sadly no shortage of examples. Thanks to the sheer number and diversity of man-made disasters, it is well-nigh impossible to encompass every aspect in a single volume such as this. Not wishing to write an encyclopaedia, I have been forced to be very selective.

The choice of what to include and what to leave out has been entirely mine. Many that I have included are not simply 'industrial' disasters.

While the reasons for structural collapses such as the Tay Bridge over a hundred years ago, and some of the countless air, marine and railway accidents in recent decades, all deserve a place in our corporate memory, it is useful to examine other kinds of catastrophe and how they might have been prevented, such as the crushings that have occurred among football crowds or fires at leisure centres such as Summerland on the Isle of Man.

In the UK alone, the tragic deaths of the young naval cadets in Chatham and the Aberfan schoolchildren, the scandal of a century of asbestos exposure, the explosions at Flixborough, Abbeystead and Buncefield, and the horrors of Piper Alpha, King's Cross and the train crash at Ladbroke Grove, to name but a few, convey lessons that we should never forget.

Abroad, some major catastrophes such as Seveso, Chernobyl and Three Mile Island have stunned the world. Lessons learnt from these are relevant to many other sectors. Understanding the underlying causes of the *Challenger* space shuttle disaster or the explosion at the Texas City oil refinery, for example, should help every director and senior manager who is trying to grapple with the challenge of changing corporate culture, regardless of the kind of business they are running.

Multiple fatalities have not been my sole criterion for disaster. A single death caused by someone else's negligence is a catastrophe for the family and friends left behind. Major pollution incidents have severely harmed our environment, great economic and social damage has been caused by the spread of animal diseases such as foot and mouth, and many people have suffered from the scandals of hospital-acquired infections or outbreaks of food poisoning.

The reader will find that each chapter briefly describes the facts, what happened and why, and what happened next, concluding with a short summary of lessons to be learned.

Finally, I discuss hazard and risk reduction, the politics of disaster and how the regulatory approach to risk control and management has developed in the United Kingdom and Europe. Too often the stable door has been shut after the horse has bolted. Yet whatever politicians say and do, the main responsibility for ensuring health and safety will always rest on company directors and managers. This book is therefore written for the directors, managers and safety professionals who follow us, in the hope that they learn something from our mistakes.

David Eves
London, 2010

Chapter 1: Too young to die

Rage, rage against the dying of the light.
(Dylan Thomas, 1914–1953)

Nothing causes more public anger than when young people's lives are cut short by carelessness or negligence.

The Marine cadets marching disaster, Chatham, England, 1951

I shall always remember the first civilian disaster that came close to me as a nine-year-old, growing up in the Medway Towns. I had often cycled down Dock Road to Chatham Naval Dockyard and was familiar with the site of the horrific road accident that occurred on the evening of 4 December 1951.

What happened?

A troop of 52 young people aged from 10 to 13, all members of the Royal Marines Volunteer Cadet Corps, led by a regular Royal Marines officer, were marching three abreast from Gillingham down Dock Road towards Chatham Dockyard where they were to attend a boxing tournament. They never made it. A local service double-decker bus ran them down in the dark, killing 24 and injuring 18. The driver realised something was wrong and pulled up some yards down the road, still unaware of what he had done.

Why?

The street lighting was very dim. The troop was marching on the left-hand side of the road with their backs towards following traffic, all wearing smart dark blue uniforms, but with no lights. It was dark and as they passed an even darker section where the street lamp was out, in spite of their wearing white belts and lanyards, the bus driver failed to pick out the marchers.

He had worked for the bus company for 40 years, 25 as a driver. The speed of the bus was later the subject of some dispute – he claimed only 15–20 mph but the officer (who had seen him coming and moved the column in towards the kerb) estimated much more. He was driving on side lights only, as was common practice at the time and not against the law, though in those conditions it would seem sensible to have used headlights too.

What happened next?

Investigations tended to be finished a lot faster than today in those immediate post-war years. An inquest was held on 14 December and the

jury returned a verdict of 'accidental death'. The coroner found that
neither the driver nor the officer leading the troop had been negligent, but
the driver was charged by the police with dangerous driving, convicted
and banned for three years and fined £20. The bus company accepted
liability and paid the parents of the dead and injured compensation
totalling £10,000.

Lessons
It was obvious that the street lighting in Dock Road was inadequate. As a
direct consequence of the tragedy, local councils embarked on a
programme to improve street lighting throughout the Medway Towns.
From then on, the armed services would always display a red light at the
rear of any columns marching anywhere at night.

Aberfan coal tip disaster, South Wales, 1966
For 50 years, millions of tons of colliery waste from Merthyr Vale coal mine
had been accumulating in several massive tips on the mountainside above
the village of Aberfan in Wales. This was an accident waiting to happen.

What happened and why?
On Friday 21 October 1966, at 9.15 in the morning, an unbelievably
horrific catastrophe occurred. A roaring avalanche of black slurry, trees,
boulders and muck surged down from a man-made mountain of colliery

waste, engulfing the junior school, part of the separate senior school, a farmhouse and 20 houses.

A deathly silence then descended, until miners hurrying from their shift change arrived and began desperately searching for survivors in the rubble. Hardly anyone was found alive. The junior school had been totally wrecked. A hundred and forty-four people, including 116 children between the ages of seven and 10, perished under the muck, among them the children and grandchildren of miners working at Merthyr Vale, tragically the very source of the destruction. Five teachers also died. Only a few minutes earlier the children had been singing 'All things bright and beautiful' in assembly.

That October, heavy rain had been falling for several days, saturating the spoil until it became completely waterlogged and unstable. Its collapse was inevitable. Ordnance Survey maps showed that tip number 7 was lying above a stream. Some previous collapses were known to have occurred but without serious consequences, which may well have contributed to the complacent attitude displayed by the colliery's management towards the safety of the tip, and their failure to foresee and prevent the tragic consequences of the slide that occurred on 21 October.

What happened next?
The mine and tip were managed by the National Coal Board (NCB), all the coal mines in Great Britain having been taken into state ownership by the postwar Labour government. There might have been some expectation that safety would have been high on the NCB's agenda, yet surprisingly the response of the Chairman of the NCB was to claim that nothing could have been done to prevent the accident.

Politically, it was essential for something to be seen to be done, and quickly. This was one of the first major disasters to be seen on national television and the general public were appalled by the tragedy.

A Tribunal of Inquiry was immediately set up under Lord Justice Edmund Davies, who heard evidence for several months. Men working on the tip said they had seen the slide begin but were unable to give any warning. A telephone line was out of order (though even had it been working, it probably would not have been much help on the day, so rapid was the collapse).

While the inquiry found the immediate cause to have been the saturation of the tip by water, which allowed fine materials to begin to flow down the mountainside, undermining and taking everything else with it, the underlying causes were found to be "ignorance, ineptitude and a failure of communication", for which the NCB was held to blame.

The NCB was required to pay £500 compensation to the families for every child lost in the disaster but no NCB employee was disciplined.

As is so often the case, an appalled and generous British public donated an enormous sum, about £20 million in today's money, to the disaster fund, indicative of their great shock at this tragic event and deep sympathy with the families. However, some of this publicly donated money was controversially used to make the tip safe, saving the NCB considerable money. Later, in 1997 the new Labour government repaid the fund some compensation, and in 2007 the Welsh Assembly donated another £2 million.

Rescuers search the slag heap that engulfed Aberfan, 21 October 1966.
Popperfoto/ Getty Images

Lessons

There had been a glaring failure to assess risk. No account had been taken of the evidence of previous slips, and geographical information on local Ordnance Survey maps about the presence of the stream beneath the tip had been ignored by a complacent management.

The safety of tips had not been covered by the Mines and Quarries Act 1954 which applied at the time. However, one positive result from this shameful calamity was the Mines and Quarries (Tips) Act 1969, which required regular inspection and maintenance of tips associated with mines and quarries. The regulatory authority, HM Mines Inspectorate (then part of the Department of Energy), began recruiting civil engineering surveyors to monitor how well the NCB complied with its duties under the new Act.

No tip disasters have since occurred in British coalfields. In 1970 Lord Robens, Chairman of the National Coal Board, went on to chair a committee that recommended sweeping changes in the regulation of health and safety at work.

Lyme Bay canoeing tragedy, Dorset, England, 1993

It doesn't take much negligence to cause a disaster. In 1993 four young people learning to canoe against the beautiful backdrop of the Dorset coast lost their lives due to a company's shocking neglect of their safety.

What happened?

An 'adventure activity' business, OLL Ltd, offered canoeing courses at a centre at Lyme Bay. On 22 March 1993 a school party was on the second day of a week's course. They were complete beginners, with only one day's previous experience in a pool in St Albans. A small group of young people, each in a kayak, paddled away from Town Beach, Lyme Regis, accompanied by two instructors. Their short voyage across the bay to Charmouth was expected to take only two hours.

But the teenagers were ill equipped for the worsening sea conditions. By the time they were a little way offshore the waves had become very threatening. One canoe soon capsized and while rescue attempts were being made by the instructors, other canoes were being swamped and swept away by the tide.

Why?

Before this tragic incident occurred, two instructors had complained to the managing director about the centre's poor safety standards and inadequate safety equipment, including the lack of flares. The instructors felt so strongly about it they resigned, saying: "We think you should take a careful look at your standards of safety, otherwise you may find yourself trying to explain why someone's son or daughter is not coming home."

He ignored their warnings.

What happened next?
The alarm was raised when the party failed to arrive at Charmouth but precious time was wasted by the centre's staff in a fruitless search before the Coastguard was alerted. A helicopter search began when a fishing boat spotted an empty canoe a couple of miles away from Lyme Bay and radioed the Coastguard. By then nearly four hours had elapsed, and while the search had continued close to shore, the survivors had drifted eight miles out to sea.

Four of the youngsters, a teacher and the two instructors managed for a while to cling to a sole remaining canoe until it, too, sank, and they were eventually found and saved, suffering from hypothermia and exhaustion. But by then four teenagers had already drowned, their life jackets waterlogged and unable to support them.

The company was prosecuted for corporate manslaughter and its managing director for manslaughter. He had been warned of the danger and was unable to explain why he had taken no action. The company was convicted and fined; the director was convicted and jailed for three years.

Lessons
In the wake of this tragedy there was strong public feeling that adventure activities needed to be properly regulated and licensed. The Health and Safety at Work etc Act clearly applied and included licensing powers. But the Health and Safety Commission, the obvious authority, was reluctant to take on the licensing of these businesses, arguing that licensing should be reserved for major hazards such as nuclear power stations and explosives factories, not for recreational activities. The government of the day sidestepped their objection and bowed to public pressure by establishing a new authority charged specifically with regulating adventure activities, the Adventure Activities Licensing Authority.

The tragic incident added weight to another campaign to change the law. A new campaigning group, Public Concern at Work, had been formed in 1993 and worked tirelessly over the next few years to introduce a law to protect whistleblowers. A Private Member's Bill was introduced, won support and was passed as the Public Interest Disclosure Act 1998, coming into effect in 1999.

The Lyme Bay canoeing tragedy led to the first conviction for corporate manslaughter in the UK.

In 2008 the Health and Safety Executive (HSE) absorbed the Adventure Activities Licensing Authority and took on its responsibilities.

Sources

Chatham cadets
Oh Mum! Oh Mum! *Time*, 17 December 1951. www.time.com/time/magazine/article/
0,9171,859447,00.html
The Times, various articles, 5 December 1951–23 January 1952

Aberfan
Davies E (chairman). *Report of the tribunal appointed to inquire into the disaster at
Aberfan on October 21st 1966* (HL 316, HC 553). London: HMSO, 1967
McLean I. *Aberfan: no end of a lesson*. History and Policy, 2006. www.historyandpolicy.
org/papers/policy-paper-52.html
Mines and Quarries (Tips) Act 1969

Lyme Bay
Activity Centres (Young Persons' Safety) Act 1995
Adventure Activities Licensing Authority. From Lyme Bay to licensing. www.aals.org.uk/
lymebay01.html
Adventure Activities Licensing Regulations 2004

Chapter 2: Flixborough, Limberg and Enschede

The catastrophic explosion at Flixborough in 1974, then the worst to have occurred in the UK since the Second World War, really deserves a chapter all of its own. It was a seminal event leading to major changes in the regulation of the chemical industry in the UK and, later, in the development of controls over major hazard plants throughout Europe. It also profoundly influenced the approach to the control of major hazards by the new British safety regulator that was to come into being just a few months after the event.

In 1972 the Robens Committee, set up by the government in 1970 to inquire into the poor state of health and safety in Great Britain, had recommended a complete overhaul of health and safety law and the establishment of a Health and Safety Commission. By the summer of 1974 a new Health and Safety at Work Bill was on its way through Parliament towards becoming law.

Flixborough, England, 1974

If any further justification were needed for raising safety standards, it came on Saturday 1 June that year, when a massive explosion occurred at a large but little-known chemical processing plant on Humberside.

What happened?

The Flixborough Works of Nypro (UK), a company formed between the National Coal Board and the Dutch State Mines, produced caprolactam, a substance used in the manufacture of nylon. It involved processing cyclohexane, a volatile and highly flammable liquid, under heat and pressure in a system of connected reactor vessels.

A crack allowing cyclohexane to escape had been discovered in one of the reactors earlier that year. The company's engineers decided to bypass the failed reactor to enable production to continue while the reactor was being repaired. They made a dog-legged length of pipework including flexible bellows in their workshop and used it to reconnect the adjoining reactors, unfortunately without having first assessed the risks and possible consequences of modifying the plant in this way, and without conducting pressure tests. These omissions were to prove fatal.

Why?

A few weeks later the bypass burst under pressure. Heated cyclohexane erupted from the plant, rapidly forming a large, uncontained cloud of flammable vapour. The vapour inevitably found a nearby source of ignition and exploded with massive force, totally destroying the factory.

A body is carried away from the remains of the Nypro works at Flixborough, 2 June 1974.
Getty Images

Had it not occurred on a Saturday, when the main office block was unoccupied, the on-site death toll might have been hundreds. As it was, 28 workers were killed and 36 injured. No one escaped alive from the adjacent control room. There the windows were blown in and the roof collapsed, killing 18.

The off-site consequences were also severe, though no one was killed. Fifty-three people were reported to have been injured and 2,000 nearby properties to have been damaged by the force of the explosion, later calculated to have released energy equivalent to 16 tonnes of TNT.

The massive blast was heard in Grimsby, many miles away. It was followed by a number of fires that continued to burn throughout the plant for several days, spreading a dirty plume of smoke across Humberside.

What happened next?
This was the first major postwar accident at a British chemical works to have had serious off-site consequences and it brought home to the public a new kind of risk that could endanger both workers and people living in the vicinity of large chemical plants.

A public inquiry was demanded and the government responded swiftly on 27 June by appointing Roger Parker QC to lead a Court of Inquiry under section 84 of the Factories Act 1961. His report was published on 12 May 1975.

Lessons
The inquiry into the disaster raised many questions, for example about modifying plant without proper regard to assessing the potential consequences, the need for pressure testing during recommissioning, the location and protection of control rooms and the need for emergency planning.

The inquiry's findings as to the technical cause of the explosion, based on an investigation by the then newly formed HSE – that it was a straightforward mechanical failure of the temporary bypass caused by a pressure surge – were to prove controversial. Arguments continued over the years, with accusations by whistleblowers of a cover-up by investigators to save the company's reputation and suggestions of more complex causes, including the possible presence of water in the reactors and the consequential build-up of excessive pressure. In 2007 the debate was still continuing, after experiments by the HSE showed that there could be some truth in that proposition.

But whatever the precise technical cause, the investigation had shown up the underlying causes: the temporary bypass had been designed by the company's own engineers who had no special expertise in high pressure pipework, no proper drawings had been prepared and there was no pressure testing of the pipework before its installation, which, to crown it all, was on temporary scaffolding that allowed the pipework to twist under pressure.

It is a common phenomenon that temporary measures are allowed to become permanent. They almost always prove inadequate. And if it leads to an escape of highly flammable vapours or liquids they will almost always find a source of ignition.

There was no prosecution. Announcing the findings of the inquiry to the House of Commons on 12 May 1975, the minister said that he had been told by the founding Director General of the HSE, John Locke, that "had this disaster occurred at a time when the provisions of the new Act were operative and effective, he would not have hesitated to go for a prosecution on indictment."

In his Annual Report of 1971, Bryan Harvey, then HM Chief Inspector of Factories, had presciently drawn attention to the growth in the size of the inventories of hazardous materials on sites in the chemical process industry. In his 1972 Report, he called for companies to notify local planning authorities so that they could consider the effects on other developments in the area. The Flixborough disaster helped to catalyse change and revolutionise the approaches both to planning and to safety management in the UK, reinforcing the political will that was already driving forward radical changes in health and safety law.

The Health and Safety at Work etc Act 1974 came into effect in January 1975. It laid new, wide-ranging duties on employers to ensure "so far as is reasonably practicable" the health and safety of their employees and to ensure the protection of the public from risks arising from the conduct of their undertaking. The courts were enabled to impose unlimited fines and even custodial sentences for certain serious offences against health and safety law, and inspectors were given powers (effective from 1 April 1975) to issue improvement and prohibition notices. If any doubters still existed, Flixborough had silenced their objections.

When the disaster occurred, I was HM District Inspector of Factories for north London, a long way from Humberside. While London did not have anywhere near the concentrations of chemical plants found in the north of England, there were a number of big plants in urban areas that had been built years earlier but were now surrounded by housing. My colleagues and I began reviewing the safety of the chemical plants on our patch with a fresh and very wary eye. The term 'major hazard' had entered the lexicon of industrial safety, and protecting the safety of the public who could be threatened by industrial accidents was beginning to become a major political issue.

The Flixborough Inquiry led to the establishment of a new Major Hazards Advisory Committee, which, over time, brought forward recommendations for controls that would require the kinds of issue raised by Flixborough to be addressed by plant operators. A framework of regulatory controls for major hazard plants in Great Britain was subsequently developed by the Health and Safety Commission over a period of years.

These controls were later extended by the European Commission in the light of the collective experience of other large-scale disasters, leading to the so-called 'Seveso Directives', and are now known in the UK as the Control of Major Accident Hazard Regulations (COMAH, last amended in 2005).

The lessons of Flixborough should never be forgotten. It was the most destructive event in the UK since the Second World War and was to remain the biggest onshore industrial explosion in the UK until the Buncefield incident in 2005.

Limberg, The Netherlands, 1975

The British were not alone in experiencing this new kind of major industrial disaster. As the new Health and Safety Commission was beginning its work in the UK, the Dutch government set up the Cobben Commission to review dangers presented by a chemical complex south of the town of Limberg. That commission had hardly begun its work before an explosion occurred at the DSM factory on 18 August 1975, killing 14 people in the control room and injuring 100 people in the vicinity of the plant.

The Cobben Commission's findings included recommendations for additional control measures, increased separation distances, and improvements in the safety of works transport specific to the DSM plant. But in spite of this experience, so similar to the UK's at Flixborough, the Dutch government stopped short of creating a Health and Safety Commission charged with developing better standards and controls. Instead they left industrial safety regulation in the hands of powerless civil servants in government departments and a multiplicity of local authorities.

The Enschede fireworks disaster, The Netherlands, 2000

The Dutch authorities were to regret this when a fireworks warehouse exploded catastrophically in the town of Enschede, exposing bureaucratic muddle and confusion about roles and responsibilities.

What happened?

On 13 May 2000 a fire at a warehouse, the SE Fireworks Depot in Enschede, caused a series of explosions that killed 22 people and injured 947. The pressure from the blasts was felt over 20 miles away and the explosions were heard at a far greater distance. Four firemen died in attempts to contain the ensuing fires, which devastated Roombeek, the immediate neighbourhood. Ten thousand people had to be evacuated. An area the size of 40 football pitches, including 15 streets, was completely destroyed and 1,250 residents were made homeless as their houses burnt down.

Why?

The fire started in a store containing 900 kg of imported fireworks in the main building. The building blew up and flames engulfed two containers which had been illegally positioned alongside it. These also exploded, causing new fires which swiftly spread to the main bunker where 177 tonnes of fireworks were stored. The whole lot blew up.

Investigators surmised that workers had propped open fire doors which, if closed, might have contained the initial fire and explosion within the main

The aftermath of the Enschede fireworks disaster, May 2000.

building. This was never confirmed. Even so, distribution of explosives between separate bunkers at safe distances should have minimised the risk of a greater catastrophe.

What happened next?

Before the explosion, the firm had been inspected by various authorities and given a clean bill of health. Arson was suspected. However, the two managers were prosecuted in 2002 for negligence causing a deadly explosion, for breaches of safety and environmental protection law and for dealing in illegal fireworks, and were sentenced to 15 months' imprisonment. In 2003 a man was sentenced to 15 years for arson in connection with the disaster.

The Enschede explosion had exposed confusion between the multiple regulatory authorities over their roles and responsibilities for licensing the fireworks depot and a weakness in local planning controls that had permitted such close proximity between housing and a major hazard.

Inevitably, the Dutch government set about tightening up the regulations relating to storage and sale of fireworks and in 2005 the European Commission amended the Seveso Directive.

Sources

Flixborough

Control of Major Accident Hazards Regulations 1999, amended 2005

European Commission. Seveso II Directive (Council Directive 96/82/EC) 1996

Factory Inspectorate. *Annual report of HM Chief Inspector of Factories*. London: HMSO, 1971 and 1972

Health and Safety Executive. *The Flixborough disaster: report of the Court of Inquiry*. London: HMSO, 1975

Enschede

After 400 homes and 15 streets are incinerated by firework blast, the Dutch ask: Was it arson? *The Independent*, 15 May 2000. www.independent.co.uk/news/world/europe/after-400-homes-and-15-streets-are-incinerated-by-firework-blast-the-dutch-ask-was-it-arson-716195.html

Video of the explosion. http://video.google.com/videoplay?docid=-6126121898177679789

Chapter 3: Deadly fires

Fire is a good servant but a bad master.
(17th-century proverb)

Legend has it that Prometheus stole fire from Zeus and brought it to mortals as a gift from the ancient gods. As a punishment for his crime, his liver was eaten by an eagle every day.

Fire is a mixed blessing. When we allow it to run out of control it can have terrifying and terrible consequences. Our carelessness has often been responsible for starting deadly conflagrations – the Great Fire of London in 1666 and the Great Chicago Fire of 1871 are memorable historical examples – but a perverse fascination with fire by some can also have fatal consequences: the raging bush fires started by an arsonist in the Australian state of Victoria in early 2009 claimed over 200 lives.

However, deliberate criminal acts are rarely behind industrial disasters. There have been many multiple fatalities in preventable industrial fires over the last 200 years and the UK has had its share. Yet in spite of all this experience, the authorities have struggled to create a framework of law which actively promotes prevention and protection. What is it about fire that makes us keep making these avoidable mistakes?

The UK's experience is by no means unique. No chapter about industrial fires would be complete without remembering a dreadful factory fire that occurred nearly a century ago in New York. It was to kick-start state regulation to raise standards of fire prevention and protection at work on both sides of the Atlantic.

The Triangle Shirtwaist factory fire, New York, 1911
In the late afternoon of Saturday 11 March 1911, 275 young women, many of them teenage girls, were looking forward to finishing their day's hard work at the Triangle Shirtwaist dressmaking factory, a nine-storey building on New York's East Side. A hundred and forty-six of them would never make it home.

What happened?
The fire started in one of the lower floors, trapping the women above. It spread rapidly upwards, consuming dress fabric and any other combustibles lying around.

Firemen outside the
Triangle Shirtwaist
factory, 25 March
1911.
Library of Congress

Why?

There were buckets of water but no effective firefighting equipment that could cope with such a rapidly spreading blaze. Means of escape were inadequate. Some doors were locked, to prevent theft of the products. Doors to the internal staircase opened inwards, causing crushes and preventing escape. Many died behind these doors. 25 bodies were later found in a cloakroom.

What happened next?

The fire department arrived quickly enough but its ladders and fire hoses could not reach the higher floors. There was an external staircase but this collapsed under the weight of panic-stricken workers desperately trying to escape, killing several more. Some women threw themselves down the lift shaft; many others jumped to their deaths from the ninth floor, thudding onto the pavement below and piling up in front of aghast onlookers.

This appalling event outraged the public. The authorities, previously reluctant to intervene and burden business with new rules and regulations, were forced to act.

Lessons

New York set up a Factory Commission, which notably included the President of the American Federation of Labor. The Commission's recommendations led to the making of fire prevention regulations which included the provision and maintenance of firefighting equipment, alarms, adequate means of escape and training of workers. All doors were to open outwards and to be kept unlocked during occupation of the building. Sprinkler systems were to be installed where more than 25 people were employed above ground level.

The owners of Triangle Shirtwaist were tried for manslaughter and acquitted: there had been no regulations for them to break. However, some lessons seem to have been learnt. Many other states soon decided to follow the example of New York and enact new safety regulations.

But regulations are one thing, observance another. In the Bronx, New York, on 25 March 1990, 79 years after the Triangle Shirtwaist disaster, 87 people were trapped and died in a fire at the Happy Land Social Club. Investigation revealed some all too familiar problems. Windows were barred, there was only one way out, there was no sprinkler system and no fire alarm.

I would like to cite just one more example from the USA before I return to our experiences of fire disasters in the UK.

Imperial Foods chicken factory fire, Hamlet, North Carolina, 1991

John Locke, the founding Director General of the HSE, sent me to the US federal Occupational Safety and Health Administration (OSHA) in 1980 to learn about its approach to safety regulation during the business-friendly, deregulatory Reagan era. When I revisited OSHA some years later, I was told about a fire that had recently occurred in a factory in North Carolina.

What happened?

The Imperial Foods chicken factory at Hamlet was just that – a factory processing poultry. It did not sound like a high fire risk. Yet 25 workers died and 54 were injured when a fire broke out in a single-storey building on 3 September 1991. The fire started in a fryer and flames and toxic fumes spread very rapidly through the factory.

Why?

The fire exits had been padlocked to prevent theft of the products and to stop workers taking unauthorised breaks.

What happened next?

Imperial Foods was fined over $800,000 for violations of safety law and its owner was sentenced to 20 years' imprisonment (he was released after serving four and a half years).

The cooker in which the fire at the Hamlet chicken factory began.
US Fire Administration

Lessons

This was another example of regulatory failure. OSHA had responsibility for enforcement of health and safety in roughly half of the states of the USA. The state of North Carolina was not one of them and it had failed for 11 years to inspect the Hamlet factory. OSHA considered using its powers under federal law to take over responsibility from the state, which then took steps to tighten up its safety laws.

The UK has had more than its share of similar disasters. Like the USA's, the UK's high standards of fire prevention and protection have been hard won by too many people's unnecessary deaths.

The Keighley fire, Yorkshire, England, 1956

When I joined HM Factory Inspectorate in the early 1960s as a trainee in the East End of London, fires and fire prevention had become very high priorities for inspectors. I soon discovered that a tragic event, the Keighley Fire, had seared the Inspectorate's collective consciousness.

In those days, the Factory Inspectorate, not the Fire Authority, was responsible for enforcement of the fire requirements of the Factories Act. The Fire Authority operated under the Fire Services Act 1947 but the two Acts were not complementary. It was not until the passing of the 1971 Fire Precautions Act that the responsibility for enforcing general fire precautions in factories was transferred to fire authorities.

Inspectors of my generation were therefore trained to look out for risks of fire and we worked closely with the fire brigades' fire prevention officers, who had an advisory role, to improve standards of fire protection and evacuation. We clearly had a mutual interest in trying to improve things.

What happened?

In February 1956 eight female workers perished, trapped behind a locked door on the top floor of a blazing Victorian woollen mill in Keighley, West Yorkshire.

Why?

The fire had been started by a plumber using a blow torch while he was installing hot water pipes in a floor below. The blow torch set fire to a rope (part of the mill shafting transmission machinery) which then acted as a wick, passing flames rapidly through openings in the oil-soaked wooden floors above. The fire spread so rapidly in the old building that witnesses later said that it "went up like a tinderbox, really quick". Fifty years later, it is still remembered in Keighley as the worst fire that has ever occurred there.

What happened next?

The mill owner was prosecuted for failure to provide a fire alarm system, whereas the principal offence should have been the locked fire exit. He was fined £15 – a low fine, said the magistrates, "because modernisation was in progress".

Lessons

After the war many UK multistorey buildings still had single staircases, no fire alarm system, and only rudimentary firefighting equipment – or even none at all. Basement rooms with only one way out were often used as workshops, and men could be found knee-deep in wood waste from saws and spindle moulding machines. Highly flammable paints and thinners were likely to be stored and used in unsuitable domestic buildings put to use as slum factories. Fire exit doors were often found locked shut for security reasons, protecting the stock rather than the workforce.

The Factory Inspectorate therefore adopted a policy of zero tolerance towards locked exits and if one were found during an inspection we would prosecute without warning. In the absence of prohibition powers until the 1974 Act, it was necessary to get a court order to close a factory down – not a quick or easy thing to do.

The tragedy at Keighley was deeply influential, both on the cultural attitude of the Inspectorate and on the development of better regulatory controls over fire. The Keighley fire and another at the William Henderson department store in Liverpool in 1960, in which 11 people died, spurred the consolidation of previous Factories Acts into the Factories Act 1961 and the passing of the Offices, Shops and Railway Premises Act 1963.

These new Acts required a certificate of adequate means of escape to be obtained by owners of multi-occupancy buildings, or by single occupiers, from the local Fire Authority, which had to be satisfied that the means of escape met certain standards. These included doors and partitions protecting escape routes being resistant to fire for half an hour, reasonable travel distances to an exit, and alternative ways out from every floor of a building.

However, the outcome was not entirely satisfactory. After this series of fatal building fires, the legislators decided to follow a strategy based on premises rather than risk, relying on inspection of the building and the issue of a certificate of 'adequate means of escape' rather than assessment of the risks from the processes. These certificates rapidly became outdated as buildings were altered. The introduction of new processes using highly flammable materials could literally render a certificate obsolete overnight.

Ironically, this worthy attempt to improve fire protection standards led to a huge increase in the installation of asbestos insulation board in older buildings, and no doubt subjected the many carpenters and joiners benefiting from this boom to considerable exposure to respirable asbestos dust. This later led to demands from trade unions for its removal because it represented an unacceptable risk to health. But no one really knows how many deaths from fire this rush to asbestos might have prevented.

It was not until it was noticed that serious fires were usually caused by processes that calls began to grow for a risk-based approach, which is where we are today.

Sources

Triangle Shirtwaist
141 men and girls die in waist factory fire. *New York Times*, 26 March 1911.
http://query.nytimes.com/gst/abstract.html?res=980CE1D61331E233A25755C2A9659C94
6096D6CF
Von Drehle D. *Triangle: the fire that changed America*. New York: Atlantic Monthly Press, 2003

Hamlet chicken factory
United States Fire Administration. *Chicken processing plant fires: Hamlet, North Carolina (September 3, 1991) and North Little Rock, Arkansas (June 7, 1991).* www.interfire.org/res_file/pdf/Tr-057.pdf
United States Occupational Safety and Health Administration. www.osha.gov.

Keighley
Tragic death blaze recalled. *Keighley News*, 24 February 2006. http://archive.keighleynews.co.uk/2006/2/24/185394.html

General
Factory Acts and Factories Acts, 1802–1961
Fire Precautions Act 1971
Fire Services Act 1947
Offices, Shops and Railway Premises Act 1963
Regulatory Reform (Fire Safety) Order 2005

Chapter 4: More conflagrations

There is no fire without some smoke.
(16th-century proverb)

Smoke inhalation is often the killer in a serious fire, but sometimes an unpredicted explosion will claim lives during firefighting.

The fire and explosion at Dudgeon's Wharf, London, 1969
In 1969 a disastrous firefighting operation in east London put the friendly, collaborative relationship that existed between the Inspectorate, the London Fire Brigade and the Fire Brigades Union under considerable strain. It remains the worst loss of UK firefighters in peacetime.

What happened?
On 17 July a fire broke out while storage tanks were being demolished by contractors at Dudgeon's Wharf, a disused tank farm on the Isle of Dogs, east London. The worst peacetime disaster to befall the London Fire Brigade (LFB) was to follow, taking the lives of five unfortunate firemen who were doing their job, attempting to make things safe.

The tank farm had been a mixed storage facility for various oils and spirits and contained more than 100 tanks with varying large capacities in a congested yard measuring about 110 yards square. Tank 97 on this site was of a welded construction with a diameter of 27 ft and a height of 35 ft. It held 125,000 gallons. Two manhole covers, one on the roof and one at ground level, were held shut with steel plates secured by nuts and bolts.

This tank had been empty for two years but had previously held myrcene, a member of the turpentine family. This chemical had left a thick, gummy deposit on the inside of the tank which could be easily ignited. When heated it would give off a flammable vapour which, if mixed with air, is potentially explosive. The word 'turps' had been chalked on the side of the tank by somebody, but not myrcene.

The details that follow illustrate just how dangerous a firefighter's job can be, particularly when dealing with the unknown. Recognising that the job would be hazardous, the demolition contractors had taken advice before starting their work. There was already a history of fires during the demolition operations at the tank farm: only a fortnight earlier 40 firemen of the LFB had been fighting a blaze on the site at a tank containing waste oil. The Brigade had attended several other fires there that had been caused by sparks from the cutting equipment being used by the demolition contractor's men.

During the morning of 17 July, the LFB was again called out, this time to a fire at tank 97. When the Brigade arrived the emergency appeared to be over. The LFB station officer in command asked about the fire situation. From what he was told he assumed that the fire was probably out but decided to make certain of this by introducing a water spray ('spray branch') into the top manhole, which had already been removed. A sub-officer and four other firemen joined the station officer on top of the tank while this operation was carried out. The local Factory Inspectorate office was telephoned to see whether they had any advice to give, but the inspector in the office was not familiar with the site and did not know what had been stored in the tank.

The station officer next decided it would be necessary to look into the tank through the bottom manhole to see if any fire was still burning and, if so, to reposition the spray branch to extinguish it. The bottom manhole cover had to be removed to do this but a spanner failed to shift the nuts; fatefully, someone suggested they should be burnt off.

As a site demolition worker set about the nuts with an oxy-acetylene burner, the station officer came down off the top to find out what was happening. Moments after the torch was applied, the tank exploded, blowing off the top and killing the five firemen who had remained there, together with a scrap metal worker.

Why?
Myrcene deposits, when heated or ignited, give off flammable vapours which, mixed with air, can be explosive. It is thought that using the spray branch had caused air to be drawn in and mixed with the flammable vapours given off by the hot myrcene deposits, so creating the conditions for the fatal explosion when the torch was applied.

What happened next?
A public inquiry was held. Clearly, if the risk had been properly understood and assessed there would have been no question of men standing on top of a tank containing flammable deposits thought likely to still be active. A lack of accurate information and a thoughtless act – the burning off of the nuts of the bottom manhole cover – led to their doom.

Lessons
The demolition of tanks that have contained flammable substances is fraught with risk. There have been many instances of tanks igniting and

exploding during cutting operations when the tanks have not been properly prepared and the operations properly conducted.

I once attempted to investigate an explosion that partially demolished an elderly couple's bungalow when an old fuel oil tank was being removed. The cowboy contractor they had innocently employed had unthinkingly used an angle grinder to disconnect the tank from the pipework. Sparks and heat generated by the grinding disc – which I found lying by the wreckage – had almost certainly caused the blast. The contractor had fled from the scene and proved to be untraceable. Fortunately no one had been hurt.

Guidance on the demolition of storage tanks that have contained flammable substances is to be found on the HSE's website.

The James Watt Street fire, Glasgow, 1968
The growing use of foamed plastic during the 1960s for upholstery or packing brought many serious fires in its wake, often in the home. Inspectors began to find very large quantities of foamed plastic being stored in upholstery factories without any regard to the dangers it presented. The substance had a propensity to burn fiercely, giving off dense clouds of poisonous fumes. Having windows barred as a security measure would add a further menace.

A fire at B Stern and Co.'s upholstery factory in James Watt Street, Glasgow was to bring these risks together with devastating consequences.

What happened and why?
On 18 November 1968, 22 upholstery workers lost their lives in an old three-storey building, a former bonded whisky warehouse, with barred windows. A fire started and the old wooden staircases were soon ablaze. A fire exit had been locked. Trapped in the inferno created by the blazing plastic, most of the victims were asphyxiated by toxic fumes. Only three people managed to escape from the building. Some were seen desperately trying to tear out the window bars with their bare hands, but their efforts were futile.

What happened next?
During the Seventies the number of serious fires involving foamed plastic began to mount. HM Factory Inspectorate, a precursor of the HSE, conducted a series of tests at the fire research facility in Borehamwood. These showed that very high concentrations of toxic gases – carbon monoxide and cyanide fumes – were rapidly released once fire took hold of this material, even when fire suppressants were added.

The James Watt
Street fire in Glasgow,
18 November 1968.
*Glasgow City
Archives and Special
Collections,
TD1431/51/47*

In 1978 I had the dubious honour of deliberately setting fire to a pile of
plastic with a page of the *Financial Times* in a demonstration of the risks
from this material at the fire services training ground in Moreton in
Marsh. A cold January fog was an unexpected bonus, with a climatic
inversion sending an evil plume of dense black smoke towards the
watching crowd of MPs, journalists and other worthies, who left
unharmed but much chastened by the alarming experience.

However, the stakes were raised again in 1980, when a fire involving
furniture containing foamed plastic trapped and killed 10 people,
including customers, on an upper floor at Woolworths in Manchester.
Several of the victims were overcome by fumes that penetrated the store's
restaurant.

Lessons
Polyurethane foamed plastic is commonly used in upholstery to improve
the comfort of armchairs and three-piece suites. The material is bulky so it
was not uncommon for very large quantities to be stored in premises
where furniture was being manufactured. Inevitably, once a fire had
started, it would be impossible to control.

It is usually smoke inhalation that kills people in a fire if they cannot get away quickly. It is vital to keep gangways and fire exits clear when flammable materials like foamed plastics are stored or used.

After these fires, Home Office would make regulations requiring all foamed plastic in furniture to be treated with fire retardants. These slow down ignition but do not prevent combustion. Once it is well alight, the plastic is just as hazardous.

The Summerland fire, Isle of Man, 1973

As we have just seen, flammable plastic materials stored or used in processes are very hazardous. And when they have been incorporated into the structure of a building that catches fire, these materials greatly increase the risks to any occupants.

The leisure industry is no stranger to disaster. A change in regulations applying to public buildings at a favourite holiday destination, the Isle of Man, was triggered by an appalling fire that occurred there in 1973.

What happened?

The Summerland Leisure Complex in Douglas was a spacious modern building designed to accommodate 10,000 visitors in dance halls, restaurants, games areas and bars. Built of concrete, it incorporated in the front and part of the roof a new translucent acrylic sheeting material called oroglas.

During the evening of 2 August a fire that was accidentally started in a kiosk by Summerland's mini-golf course spread to the main building, where about 3,000 people were enjoying themselves.

Why?

The fire caught hold of the acrylic sheeting which acted as a fuel, melting and burning fiercely. Flames then spread rapidly across the interior of the roof, fed by oxygen entering from numerous unprotected vents in the building which were now acting as chimneys.

The melting, burning plastic material began dropping onto the heads of the people below, causing panic and confusion and starting more fires. Instead of an orderly evacuation people simply ran for their lives, some finding themselves trapped by locked doors while burning material continued to rain down on them. A dangerous crush occurred as many people rushed to escape through the main entrance. Fifty-one of the centre's occupants failed to make it to safety outside.

What happened next?
Half an hour passed before the fire brigade arrived, as in the panic no one at the scene had thought to call them. Fortunately, the huge blaze was seen by a ship out at sea and the skipper reported it to the Coastguard, who alerted the brigade.

A public inquiry was held during the next six months and decided that the deaths were due to misadventure. No individual was blamed for the fire but the disorderly evacuation and use of highly flammable materials in the building's construction were strongly criticised.

In light of the inquiry's recommendations substantial changes were made to the Isle of Man's building regulations concerning the structural design of large public buildings and the use of fire-resistant materials.

The King's Cross fire, London, 1987
Fires at London Underground stations at Green Park and Oxford Circus had fortunately not led to loss of life, but these were followed by a truly horrific fire at King's Cross Underground station.

What happened?
On the evening of 18 November 1987, 31 people, chiefly members of the public but including a firefighter, died in a fire that raged up the escalator shaft and into the ticket hall from below while scores of people were entering the station for their journeys home.

Why?
A wooden escalator had caught fire when combustible rubbish that had accumulated beneath it was ignited, probably by a discarded burning cigarette end (smoking was still permitted on the Tube). There was a rush of air up the escalator shaft, with flames feeding on the paintwork and causing the fire to flash up towards the ticket hall above.

What happened next?
A public inquiry was set up under the chairmanship of Mr Desmond Fennell QC to find out what had happened and make recommendations to prevent a recurrence. The hearing lasted many weeks.

Lessons
The Tube had suffered from under-investment for many years. The Fennell Report's recommendations led to new regulations and a wave of investment in safety measures, such as the replacement of all wooden escalators on the Underground, the installation of automatic sprinklers and heat detectors in escalators, and fire safety training for station staff.

The burnt-out ticket hall after the fire at King's Cross Underground station, 18 November 1987
David Eves

Camberwell, London, 2009

Even so, we still have more to learn about fires. In July 2009 a tragic blaze in Camberwell, London, opened a new debate.

What happened?

On 3 July six people, including three small children, perished in a fire in a 12-storey council block containing 98 flats.

Why?

The fire broke out on the ninth floor and spread rapidly to the floors above and below. There was only a single staircase and this quickly filled with smoke, preventing escape. There was no fire alarm and no sprinkler system, although smoke detectors were fitted in the flats.

What happened next?

Firefighters arrived within minutes and managed to rescue 40 people. Unfortunately the intensity and unusually rapid spread of the fire prevented six others from being saved. The rescue service was unable to use ladders above the height of the ninth floor, normally depending on modern design features, such as dry risers, to assist in firefighting in tall buildings. Seven floors of the building were severely damaged.

Lessons

The fire has raised important questions about the design of tall buildings and fighting fires. The Communities and Local Government minister has

ordered a review by the government's chief fire and rescue adviser "to
ensure any lessons could be shared quickly with fire and rescue
authorities, landlords and tenants". The terms of reference include the 'fire
safety matters applicable to this building' and 'operational procedures'.
The findings of his review are awaited.

More generally, it is clear that lessons about controlling risks from fire
have been learnt painfully slowly over the 100 years or so that have
passed since the Triangle Shirtwaist fire. The development of today's high
standards has been a slow, evolutionary process in the light of much bitter
experience.

It was eventually agreed by policy makers that certificates of adequate
means of escape in case of fire relating to buildings quickly became out of
date and needed to be replaced by a more flexible system of assessment
that took account of a range of risk factors such as building design and
usage. Since the Regulatory Reform (Fire Safety) Order 2005, the
occupiers of industrial premises and local authority owners of residential
accommodation have had a duty to carry out an assessment themselves of
any risk of fire appropriate to the particular circumstances, and then take
appropriate measures to manage the risks they have identified. After the
Camberwell fire, it became clear that a number of housing authorities
needed to accelerate their programmes and complete these assessments.

Sources

Dudgeon's Wharf
Dudgeon's Wharf – 17th July 1969. www.fireservice.co.uk/history/dudgeonswharf.php
Report of a Public Inquiry into a fire at Dudgeons Wharf on 17th July 1969 (Cmnd 5034).
London: HMSO, 1970

James Watt Street
The James Watt Street fire. www.sunnygovan.com/PLACES/Places/
JamesWattStreetFire.html

Summerland
Isle of Man Fire Brigade. The Summerland fire disaster, 2nd August 1973.
www.iomfire.com/main/Summerland.htm
Summerland Fire Commission. *Summerland Fire Commission Report*. Douglas: Isle of
Man Government Office, 1974

King's Cross
Fennell D. *Investigation into the King's Cross Underground fire*. London: HMSO, 1988

Camberwell

Lakanal House: new evidence reveals how fatal fire spread. *The Architects' Journal* online, 8 July 2009. www.architectsjournal.co.uk/news/daily-news/lakanal-house-new-evidence-reveals-how-fatal-fire-spread/5204724.article

Six killed in tower block blaze. BBC News Online, 3 July 2009. http://news.bbc.co.uk/1/hi/england/london/8133871.stm

General

Department of Communities and Local Government. www.communities.gov.uk

Chapter 5: Gas explosions

As a Chief Engineer of British Gas once said to me, "You can't take the bang out of gas." Only prevention of leaks can avoid fatal explosions.

During the 1960s there had been a series of explosions under the streets of various British towns caused by gas leaking from the Victorian gas mains laid a century or more earlier. The length of the network was vast: they had laid down enough pipes to go four times round the globe. These mains were largely cast iron pipes, susceptible over the years to corrosion in damp ground or brittle fracture from movement or compacting of the ground by increasingly heavy vehicular traffic. The gas itself, previously locally supplied 'town gas' manufactured in the local gas works, was being replaced by natural gas from the North Sea pumped at higher pressures, but this was not the real problem. Like so much of Great Britain's postwar infrastructure, the cast iron mains distribution system was long overdue for replacement.

After explosions that occurred over the Christmas and New Year holiday period in 1976/77, the Secretary of State for Energy commissioned a report by Dr P J King, who made recommendations for mains replacement to reduce the risk of leaks and explosions. British Gas, then the state-owned monopoly supplier of mains gas to industry and the general public and effectively the self-regulator of gas safety, responded with a nationwide programme of replacement, sometimes using ductile iron which could withstand traffic movement better than cast iron, but more often using plastic piping made from polyethylene. Corrosion-free and resilient, this had the added benefit of being capable of insertion into existing pipework. The yellow plastic pipes stacked at the roadside soon became a familiar sight as the years went on.

The task was truly enormous but the huge investment certainly began to reduce the risk of explosions. Gas detector vans combing the streets for leaks were another element of the strategy, enabling prioritisation of the programme towards higher risks.

British Gas was soon to be successfully privatised, while the HSE was given the task of regulating gas safety, and everything seemed to be going along pretty well.

The explosion at Putney, London, 1985
However, a major catastrophe in London in 1985 was to galvanise both the authorities and the industry into the realisation that the ageing cast

iron mains were continuing to deteriorate and that the speed of
replacement was too slow.

What happened and why?
At breakfast time on 10 January 1985 the whole country was shocked
when private flats in Putney were destroyed in a gas explosion which
killed eight residents.

Gas was supplied to the flats for cooking and heating via a service pipe
buried underground, connected to an underground low-pressure cast iron
main. Over time the main had been cracked by the weight of traffic
passing over it, allowing gas to escape into the soil. It seeped slowly
through the soil into the void where the service pipe lay and entered the
building, where it mixed with air and formed an explosive concentration.

While the source of ignition was never identified with certainty, it is likely
to have been the firing up of a central heating boiler or lighting of a gas
ring that triggered the fatal explosion.

What happened next?
Only a few days earlier, the HSE had taken over responsibility for
enforcing domestic gas safety from British Gas, which had been used to
regulating itself. It was an unfortunate beginning to the HSE's new role,
but it also presented an opportunity to show how an independent
regulator might make a difference to protection from gas explosions.

I went to the scene to see for myself how our investigation was proceeding.
Much to the dismay of British Gas, which had its own laboratories, we took
possession of the pipework and examined it carefully in our own Health
and Safety Laboratory in Sheffield. It soon became clear that the fracture of
the cast iron pipe was not at all unusual and that similar circumstances were
likely to arise elsewhere. Pressure now mounted on British Gas to accelerate
its programme of mains gas replacement and, to its credit, it did.

Even so, the accelerated replacement programme would still take years to
complete. Inevitably, more accidents would occur. Another soon caused
multiple fatalities at Rutherglen, Glasgow, where five members of the
public were killed. Like Putney, that explosion was again caused by a leak
from a cast iron main that had been cracked by traffic.

Lessons
It was clear that a major national problem existed. The tragic events at
Putney and Rutherglen in 1985 had a profound influence on the attitude
of the gas industry's new regulator, the HSE. It took some time for

legislation to bite, but as gas leaks continued to occur, by 1996 regulations had been made to address the risks from pipelines.

The Larkhall gas explosion, Scotland, 1999

New factors came to light in a tragic incident in Lanarkshire. This time the findings of the investigation would lead to proceedings in the Scottish courts and a heavy penalty.

What happened and why?

On 22 December 1999 a gas explosion destroyed a bungalow at Larkhall, Lanarkshire, killing its four inhabitants – two parents and their two young children. A mains gas leak was immediately suspected as the cause. This time shock was followed by public outrage.

Like the event at Putney, gas had migrated from a leaking main into domestic premises, where it inevitably found a source of ignition.

What happened next?

Again, the HSE investigators took possession of the suspect piping and examined it in the Sheffield laboratory. It was soon evident that the medium pressure ductile iron main had not been adequately protected against corrosion and that neglect to do this had resulted in the leak that caused the explosion. Emphasis had hitherto been placed on replacing the brittle and corrosion-prone Victorian cast iron pipework, and in parts of the country since the 1960s replacements were being carried out using ductile iron pipework. If this is to resist corrosion damage from exposure to damp and acid conditions, it has to be properly protected.

BG Transco – the successor to British Gas with responsibility for maintaining the UK's 270,000 km of gas mains – was prosecuted in the Sheriff Court for a breach of health and safety law; essentially, the company was accused of failing to ensure safety in the way it conducted its undertaking, the supply of gas. It was found guilty, heavily criticised by the Sheriff and fined a record £1.2 million.

Lessons

Larkhall had been yet another wake-up call. In September 2000 Transco agreed to replace all medium-pressure ductile iron mains within 30 metres of buildings by 2002. The HSE then reviewed the current rate of progress on the replacement programme with Transco and found that, in spite of all the work, the annual rate of corrosion or fracture accidents had actually increased slightly since 1977 – averaging about three or four major incidents and causing one or two deaths per year.

In September 2001 a further acceleration of the mains replacement programme to replace all cast iron as well as ductile iron gas mains located within 30 metres of buildings was therefore announced. This meant that the remaining 91,000 km of iron mains would be replaced within the next 30 years. There is still scope for further accidents but as the programme continues, the risk should steadily diminish.

The ICL Stockline explosion, Glasgow, 2004

> "...an avoidable tragedy..." (Lord Gill)

Fractured gas mains are not the only gas pipeline hazard that can lead to disastrous consequences. An explosion at a factory in 2004 was Scotland's worst industrial disaster since the *Piper Alpha* explosion and fire in 1988.

The unhappy history of management disregard and ineffectual regulatory intervention that led up to the explosion, the outcome of the HSE's investigation, and the findings of the subsequent public inquiry are worthy of close examination. There are many lessons here.

What happened?
The ICL companies ICL Plastics Ltd and ICL Tech Ltd – also known as 'Stockline' – had used Grovepark Mills in Maryhill, Glasgow, since 1968

The aftermath of the ICL Stockline explosion at Maryhill, Glasgow, 11 May 2004.
Health and Safety Laboratory

to manufacture plastic products. One of the three buildings was originally a weaving mill dating from Victorian times. This main building was brick built, with a basement, ground floor and three upper storeys.

At midday on 11 May 2004 an explosion occurred in the basement. The pressure wave blew out the basement ceiling – a heavy steel and concrete structure – and the walls of the ground floor coating and despatch area, causing the total collapse of the floors above.

Crushed under tons of rubble, nine people died and 40 were seriously injured, including a member of the public. Survivors were being pulled from the wreckage by local residents as the emergency services arrived.

Why?

The explosion was caused by a leak of liquefied petroleum gas (LPG), propane, which was kept in a storage tank outside in the yard to supply gas ovens used in the manufacturing processes.

The propane gas was piped into the basement through piping that had been buried underground as long ago as 1969. The buried piping had corroded and began to leak gas which, heavier than air, eventually found its way into the basement. On 11 May enough had accumulated and mixed with air to form an explosive atmosphere and cause the catastrophic explosion, probably ignited by an electrical spark. (The ignition source was not firmly established by the subsequent investigation.)

What happened next?

Responding to public anger, the HSE and Strathclyde Police quickly launched a joint investigation, reporting to the Area Procurator Fiscal. Their work was supported by forensic scientists from the Health and Safety Laboratory.

It emerged that over the years before the explosion, risk assessments had never included examining the condition of the underground pipes. One risk assessment had even been carried out by a student during vacation work.

The HSE had recommended excavating the gas pipes in 1988 but this advice was not followed up, by either the management or the regulator. It was not clear for how long the gas had been leaking.

While other possible sources of fuel for the explosion were considered, such as dust, flammable solvents or naturally occurring gas, the investigation showed beyond doubt that the source was LPG that had leaked from the corroded underground piping close to the basement wall and that it had not been properly installed or maintained.

A report was sent in 2005 to the Procurator Fiscal, who decided to prosecute both of the associated ICL firms. They pleaded guilty at the High Court in Glasgow to breaches of health and safety law concerning failure to ensure the safety of their employees and others, in that they failed to carry out a suitable and sufficient risk assessment or have a proper system to inspect and maintain the LPG pipe. The judge, Lord Brodie, likened the situation to a "ticking time bomb" and fined each company £200,000, remarking that whatever fine was imposed, it would never satisfy the victims' families.

Following the successful prosecution, public outrage did not diminish. Demands for a public inquiry led by the local MP and the victims' families were accepted by the Scottish authorities, and Lord Gill, Lord Justice Clerk and the second most senior judge in Scotland, was appointed to conduct it.

The inquiry opened on 8 April 2008. It gradually became clear that over a long period managers had ignored advice from the HSE in 1988 that the underground pipework should be excavated. Unfortunately, the recommendation had not been followed up effectively by the regulator. At the close of the inquiry the HSE expressed regret that its intervention had not been more successful.

As so often, there were numerous factors which led to the circumstances in which this had become an accident waiting to happen. While the technical cause of the disaster was clear enough, Lord Gill's year-long inquiry also exposed a number of underlying causes. His findings are worth quoting in full:

> The underground ageing metallic LPG pipe was out of sight and out of mind; it was inadequately protected when buried, it was subject to corrosion and ultimately it failed; the management of the ICL companies lacked knowledge and understanding that LPG is heavier than air and when escaping will track to accumulate at the lowest point in drains, ducts and voids, presenting the danger of an explosion; when the yard was raised in 1973 and later, when the chequer plate floor was laid over the open pit area, the LPG safety implications were overlooked; no consideration was given to the presence of LPG on the premises and the existence of the void within the building; the risks posed were not identified and not understood; opportunities to consider the continuing integrity of the buried pipe were missed; the Inquiry has identified serious weaknesses in the existing health &

safety regime arising from the complexity of the legislation and a lack of effective communication between HSE, UKLPG, suppliers and users on safety issues; and deficiencies in HSE's oversight of ICL in failing to appreciate the significance of buried pipe work, failing to pursue follow up visits promptly and lacking caution in the acceptance of a compromise put forward in respect of a recommendation it made that the buried pipe work be excavated to ascertain its condition.

Lessons

This was a damning indictment of all concerned. As we have already seen from the descriptions of other gas-related disasters, buried metallic pipework is at risk from corrosion, shifting ground, vibration from passing vehicles or damage during site alterations. Risk assessments should take account of all this.

Lord Gill's report made a number of recommendations addressed to the wider industry and the regulator, aimed (rather narrowly because of the limitations of his terms of reference) at streamlining the regime applying to buried metallic pipework carrying LPG in the form of vapour, and minimising the chances of a recurrence of an event like that at ICL. But much of what he said could equally be applied to pipe work carrying LPG as a liquid.

As he remarked, "Out of sight should never mean out of mind." Among his numerous recommendations, he pointed out that effective arrangements need to be made for the maintenance, renewal or repositioning of any buried pipes. Risk assessments should include the risk of leakage of flammable gases from tanks, cylinders, valves, pipes and fittings whether under or above ground. There needed to be a system to inspect these periodically.

Buried metallic pipes should be effectively corrosion-protected and maintained. Alternatively, they may be replaced either with pipes above ground or buried plastic pipes constructed and installed to the appropriate standards.

But by now, over five years had elapsed since the explosion. Lord Gill also commented that: "The factors involved are not atypical of users of bulk storage LPG more widely... As matters now stand, there is every possibility that a similar disaster could occur again."

He was very concerned that the HSE had still not produced a coherent action plan to deal with underground metallic pipework and the risk of a recurrence. Criticising the lack of vigour shown by the authorities and the industry, he set out one of his own, saying: "While the probability of another explosion may be low, the consequences of a similar event, should it occur, may be catastrophic. A sense of urgency would be an appropriate response to the serious issue of public confidence that this disaster has raised."

Lord Gill went on to comment on the costs and benefits of his proposals, essentially saying that when balanced against the potential risks, the costs of implementation were not unreasonable. The HSE responded publicly in a press release on 16 July 2009. Apologising to the victims and their families that its intervention at ICL had not been brought to a successful conclusion, it said that as a result of the investigation it had been developing with LPG suppliers and their trade association a plan to replace all underground metal pipework for carrying LPG with more robust plastic pipes. The industry had signed up to this and it was now being actively pursued.

Lord Gill made it clear that in this case the regulator shares some responsibility for its failure to follow up its recommendations with effective enforcement action when it should have been plain that its advice was likely to be ignored. The supplier of the gas did not escape criticism either. Nevertheless, Lord Gill rightly emphasised that the primary responsibility for LPG safety continues to lie with the person who creates the risk. It was said later that it would have cost only £405 to replace the corroded pipework at Grovepark Mills.

Sources

Putney
HM Factory Inspectorate. *The Putney explosion*. London: HMSO, 1985
HM Factory Inspectorate. *The Rutherglen explosion: a report of the investigation by the Health and Safety Executive into the explosion on 29 November 1985 at Kingsbridge Drive, Rutherglen, Glasgow*. London: HMSO, 1986

Larkhall
House blast victims named. BBC News Online, 22 December 1999. http://news.bbc.co.uk/1/hi/scotland/575447.stm

ICL Stockline
The ICL Inquiry. www.theiclinquiry.org
The ICL Inquiry report. Explosion at Grove Park Mills, Maryhill, Glasgow, 11 May 2004 (HC 838). Edinburgh: The Stationery Office, 2009. www.theiclinquiry.org/Documents/Documents/HC838ICL_Inquiry_Report.pdf

Chapter 6: Ignorance is not blissful

Where ignorance is bliss / 'Tis folly to be wise
(Thomas Gray, 1716–1771)

As the saying goes, "You don't know what you don't know", but proper identification of hazards and competent assessment of risks goes a long way towards reducing uncertainty. Many disasters have occurred where there has been a failure to identify a hazard and foresee the risk it presents.

The explosion at Abbeystead, Lancashire, England, 1984

On 23 May 1984 a bizarre explosion occurred in the village of Abbeystead in the tranquil surroundings of the Forest of Bowland, Lancashire, an area of outstanding natural beauty.

Local residents had been concerned about the flooding that had occurred for many years during the winter in the lower valley of the river Wyre. In response, North West Water, the local water authority, had commissioned a scheme to regulate the flow of the rivers Lune and Wyre, known as the Lune/Wyre Transfer Scheme.

Some time after the scheme had come into operation (and some years had elapsed between the commissioning of the design and its completion) the water authority decided to reassure the residents and allay their concerns about the risk of flooding by inviting them to attend a demonstration of how the flow of the two rivers could now be controlled by transferring water from one to the other. A group of 44 people, including some of the authority's staff, accordingly gathered on 23 May at the pump house (known as a 'valve house') situated at the outfall end of the scheme at Abbeystead, to see how it worked.

A tunnel several miles long known as the Wyresdale Tunnel had been constructed between the two rivers, enabling flows to be regulated whenever necessary by transferring water between them using pumps situated in the valve house. This had been built of concrete and carefully concealed, with its roof covered and grassed over for environmental reasons.

What happened?

As the scheme was being explained to the assembled party, the pumps were deliberately started and began transferring water into the River Wyre. What followed was unexpected and unimaginable. Survivors described an intense flash of light followed by a mighty explosion which utterly wrecked the pump house.

Sixteen people were killed and 28 injured. No one present escaped unhurt. Victims not killed by the explosion were crushed to death or injured by falling sections of the concrete roof blown asunder by the blast.

Why?

A gas explosion was immediately suspected by the HSE. They sensibly enlisted the aid of British Coal to ventilate the tunnel with powerful fans used in deep mining to clear it of any gas that might be lingering.

It was not immediately apparent, but later became clear, that methane occurring naturally in the hillsides – where coal had once been mined – had become entrained in water seeping through the tunnel's concrete lining and gathering in the tunnel itself. For 17 days beforehand no pumping of water had taken place, and gas had unknowingly been allowed to build up in a void.

When the pumps were started a deadly mixture of gas and air was pushed along the tunnel towards the pump house. Inevitably the gas and air, now mixed within the limits of explosibility, found a source of ignition and exploded with enormous force. The source was never established with certainty but was likely to have been an electrical spark or the lighting of a cigarette by one of the visitors. Smoking had not been prohibited.

What happened next?

The HSE published a report of their technical investigation which I helped present at a press conference in Manchester. Its findings satisfied the public's expectation of an explanation for this bizarre tragedy.

Compensation claims totalling up to £4 million were later lodged against the water authority (the client and operator), the contractor and the firm of consulting engineers who had designed and supervised the building of the pumping station. All were initially found liable but judges at an appeal court hearing decided finally that sole liability rested on the consulting engineers.

There was no criminal prosecution under health and safety law as the design of the pump house had preceded the 1974 Act.

Lessons

I can do no better than quote from my former HSE colleagues' statement about the Abbeystead explosion, which is to be found on the HSE webpage for COMAH Safety Report Assessment guidance. They draw attention there to several failings in technical measures:

The possibility of a methane rich environment had not been recognised. The fact that large quantities of methane might be dissolved in water, which subsequently leaked into the system, was not considered by those involved with the design/operation of the system. A system designed for discharging water open to the atmosphere would have prevented an explosion. The operation of the plant was not in accordance with the operating manual provided by the designers of the systems. Changes in the operating procedures had taken place without proper consultation as to their impact.

Operators were not fully aware of the significance of special features of the pumping installation.

Essentially, a well-intentioned attempt to reassure the public that a risk was under control had backfired with tragic consequences. There had been a failure to foresee the methane risk in spite of available evidence, flaws in design, and a desire to preserve the appearance of the local environment, leading to a lack of adequate ventilation. There was also a failure to understand the need to follow laid-down operating procedures that – in spite of all the foregoing factors – might still have avoided the fateful combination of circumstances that occurred on that springtime evening.

The jet fire at Hickson and Welch Limited, Yorkshire, England, 1992
On 21 September 1992 the HSE's Area Director in Leeds telephoned me to report that a catastrophe had just occurred at a chemical works in Yorkshire, possibly the most serious incident since Flixborough. We set an investigation in train immediately.

What happened?
Hickson and Welch Ltd was a chemical manufacturing company of long standing and a major employer in the Yorkshire town of Castleford. The company had decided that a batch still that had been installed in the nitrotoluenes area of the plant in 1961 was to be cleaned of accumulated residues – the first time this had been done in 30 years.

A tarry sludge of residue some 14 inches deep had been measured at the bottom of the still and reported to management, who assumed it consisted of a thermally stable tar. Neither the sludge nor the vessel's atmosphere was analysed. The operators were told to apply steam to the bottom of the vessel to soften the sludge, and this was done. The residue could then be raked out manually through a manhole opening, accessible from a scaffolding platform.

Several men began cleaning the still, working from the scaffold, using metal rakes. After about an hour the vessel's temperature gauge was seen

The gutted office block at Hickson and Welch after the explosion, 21 September 1992.
David Eves

in the control room some distance away to be reading 48° C. The men were told to cut off the steam, and did so.

By around 1.20, during lunchtime, most of the men had left the raking job and only one man remained on the scaffold. He stopped raking when he noticed a blue light inside the still, which immediately turned orange. He leapt for his life from the scaffold as a jet of flame suddenly roared out of the manhole, wrecking the scaffold and hurling the manhole cover into the centre of the control building. Like a giant blowtorch, the horizontal flame destroyed the control room and played against the wall of the main office block 55 metres away, setting it on fire. Simultaneously, burning vapours jetted upwards from the vessel's rear top vent.

The jet fire is estimated to have lasted one minute before subsiding from lack of fuel, but by then several other fires had started. These were extinguished by the local fire brigade, who attended with 22 appliances and over 100 firefighters.

Sadly, it was discovered that two workers had been killed in the control room, their escape impeded by an inward opening door. Two other men who escaped from the room died later from the burn injuries they had suffered while escaping. In the office block the body of a woman was found in the lavatories where she had been overcome by smoke. Fortunately, no one else was in the offices during lunchtime. Several vehicles in the car park were burnt out.

Why?

The investigation by the HSE found that a number of factors had conspired to create this disaster:

- The vessel had not been cleaned for 30 years, and due to a reorganisation no one present had any knowledge or experience of the required cleaning operation.
- The sludge and vessel atmosphere were not analysed before the cleaning operation began.
- The sludge was incorrectly assumed to be thermally stable. In fact the vapours it gave off were flammable.
- The sludge temperature was inaccurately measured, by the positioning of the temperature probe.
- The steam supply was at a higher temperature than intended because of a faulty pressure reducing valve.
- Permit-to-work systems were not properly in place (permits had been issued for removal of the manhole cover and for blanking off the inlet at the vessel's base, but not for the raking out).
- The vessel inlet was not isolated before cleaning began.
- A metal rake was an unsuitable tool for cleaning a vessel containing flammable materials and vapour.
- The positions of the control room and office block put them at risk from a fire or explosion in the plant.

What happened next?

The incident was, at the time, the worst to have occurred in the chemicals industry since Flixborough, but in the light of the HSE's thorough investigation it was decided that there was no need for a public inquiry. The company was prosecuted and fined £250,000 for breaches of health and safety law.

Lessons

As at Flixborough, the control room had been located in a vulnerable position. At any chemical factory, regular cleaning of plant and equipment has to be an essential part of a maintenance programme. Procedures and safe systems of work have to be properly documented to maintain the corporate memory of what has to be done, when, and how.

After the investigation, the Secretary of State for Employment was given a presentation by the HSE about what had caused the Hickson and Welch disaster. In this case, due to recent organisational changes, the cleaning operation was being carried out by an inexperienced team reporting to an overworked manager. Problems can be created by management of change that has not taken factors like these properly into account.

At the time, terms like 'downsizing', 'rightsizing', 'multitasking' and other means of running businesses more efficiently had become fashionable phrases and were the latest manifestations of a difficult economic period. The minister was given food for thought when he was told that one of the root causes of the disaster had been a loss of corporate memory due to organisational changes involving reductions in the number of experienced, knowledgeable staff.

Ignorance of risk is certainly not blissful.

Sources

Abbeystead

Health and Safety Executive. *The Abbeystead explosion: a report of the investigation by the Health and Safety Executive into the explosion on 23 May 1984 at the valve house of the Lune/Wyre Water Transfer Scheme at Abbeystead.* Sudbury: HSE Books, 1985

Hickson and Welch

Health and Safety Executive. *The fire at Hickson and Welch Limited. A report of the investigation by the Health and Safety Executive into the fatal fire at Hickson and Welch Limited, Castleford on 21 September 1992.* Sudbury: HSE Books, 1994

Chapter 7: Seveso and other environmental calamities

Give me liberty. I've already got death.
(Sign displayed by a resident of Love Canal, 1978)

Multiple fatalities always catch headlines but so too do major pollution incidents that have seriously damaged the environment (and sometimes people). The infamous disaster at Seveso falls within this category but the others that I have chosen to include here will be less well known. There are lessons to be drawn from each of them.

Love Canal, New York State, 1970s

A small community in Niagara Falls, New York State, became a *cause célèbre* after it was discovered that it had been built over a chemical waste tip that had been sold for one dollar. It was some time before it became clear that this was not value for money.

What happened and why?

Soon after the Second World War was over, the Hooker Electrochemical Company disposed of about 40,000 tonnes of chemical waste in a clay-lined canal, which it then covered permanently – or so it thought. The company later sold the land to the Niagara School Board for one dollar. The deeds mentioned that chemicals had been buried there but these were left unspecified and soon forgotten.

A community, Love Canal, sprang up on and around the site. Problems began to emerge in the 1970s: first, there were simply unpleasant smells but then some people began to suffer skin rashes. Things got a lot worse after exceptional rainfall brought chemicals to the surface. The local water supply and surface soil became heavily contaminated and the atmosphere grew foul as the unidentified chemicals gave off toxic fumes. A number of people became seriously ill.

What happened next?

Local residents were evacuated for their safety while an investigation was launched. By 1978 it was clear that a scandalous state of affairs had been allowed to exist. The US President, Jimmy Carter, announced a 'federal health emergency' and allocated funds for the Federal Disaster Assistance Agency to help Niagara Falls to clean up the site. It was the first time that federal emergency funds had ever been provided for this kind of disaster.

Love Canal would remain a byword for environmental deception in the
USA. It was suspected that many similar dumps of toxic chemical existed,
as yet undetected.

Seveso, Italy, 1976

In 1976 a disaster that occurred in Italy was to become a milestone in the
development of European safety and environmental legislation.

What happened?

The Icmesa Chemical Company manufactured herbicide in its works outside
the small town of Seveso in northern Italy. Around lunchtime on Saturday
9 July 1976, the maintenance shift heard a strange whistling sound and
noticed white vapour escaping from a roof vent. This lasted about 20
minutes, by the end of which time a large, dense white cloud was drifting
high in the sky over Seveso towards Milan, about 15 miles away.

Why?

A runaway reaction had caused a 'bursting disc' to rupture, releasing the
contents of a reactor vessel to the atmosphere. The disc, designed to
relieve excessive pressure, had been set for a much higher pressure than
would normally ever be reached in the reactor.

However, earlier that Saturday there had been an interruption during the
distillation of a batch of product. This had resulted in the mixture being
held in the reactor vessel for much longer than usual, without any stirring

or cooling of its contents. The plant operators had also deviated from operating procedure by acidifying the mixture after distillation rather than before. The combined effects led to an exothermic reaction, overheating of the mixture and overpressurisation of the reactor vessel.

What happened next?

After about an hour the operators were able to inject cooling water and stop the runaway reaction. The crisis appeared to be over.

However, the substances that had been released contained a small quantity of TCDD, a highly toxic dioxin. After the contaminated cloud had passed over Seveso and its population of 17,000, a large number of people soon felt very unwell. Many were later diagnosed as suffering from chloracne, a skin complaint caused by exposure to chemicals. Fortunately no one died but many rabbits and poultry were found to have perished in the nearby fields.

Large scale slaughtering of animals was then undertaken to prevent any toxic substances entering the food chain. Later some pregnant women aborted their babies, fearing deformities.

Eventually five employees of Icmesa and its parent company were prosecuted, convicted and sentenced to jail terms. Three of them successfully appealed against their convictions. Icmesa paid civil compensation to victims and the Italian government found a substantial sum for the cleaning up of the widespread land contamination, an operation that has taken many years.

Lessons

At first it was not at all clear to the authorities what had happened. Communications with the company were almost non-existent and there was a lack of information about the substances that had been released and their associated hazards. Confusion reigned for some days.

As well as the operators' deviation from normal procedure that had sown the seeds of disaster, it later became apparent that several other factors had led up to the accidental discharge of highly poisonous material and then the failure to mitigate its consequences. For example, if the reactor's relief disc had been set at a lower pressure the temperature and pressure within the reactor would not have risen so high and the consequences of the disc bursting would not have been so severe, particularly as there should also have been a means of capturing the discharge by diverting it to another vessel before it could escape from the building. This had been recommended but never implemented, which says little for the safety culture at the plant.

Moreover, there was no automatic control system on the plant nor any sensors linked to alarms that might have alerted operators to abnormality in time to prevent the runaway reaction. Emergency planning had made no provision for warning the local population or giving useful information about the chemicals and hazards to the emergency services.

Even today the toxic effects of small quantities of dioxins on humans remain controversial (TCDD had been used in high concentrations in the Vietnam War, where it was known as 'Agent Orange') but there was no doubting that it had caused the many cases of chloracne in Seveso. Seveso was an entirely preventable disaster. It was a wake-up call to the European Commission, leading over the years to a series of European Directives bearing its name, implemented in the UK by the Control of Major Accident Hazards Regulations (COMAH). As this law is intended to cover both environmental protection and the safety of people, the Environment Agency and the HSE are jointly responsible as the UK's 'competent authority' for investigating major accidents to which the Directive applies and reporting their findings to the European Commission.

Nearly 30 years after the disaster at Seveso, this partnership was successfully put to the test in the Buncefield investigation.

Sandoz, Switzerland, 1986
Europe learnt a new lesson about the hazards of firefighting when a fire occurred at a chemical works on the upper reaches of the River Rhine. The consequences were felt as far away as the river's estuary on the North Sea.

What happened and why?
The Rhine was heavily polluted with toxic chemicals when a fire occurred at the Sandoz chemical works near Basel, Switzerland, on 1 November 1986.

In order to bring the fire under control, huge volumes of water had to be used. The site was not bunded at the perimeter and the 'firewater' ran off into the river, heavily contaminated by toxic chemicals. About 30 tonnes of pesticides were washed away.

What happened next?
Fourteen people were treated for inhalation of toxic fumes but no one was killed. However, hundreds of thousands of fish were poisoned and the Rhine turned red. It took about ten days for the contaminated water to reach the mouth of the river.

Lessons

Risk assessments for sites storing large quantities of toxic chemicals need to take account of the risk of contaminated water running off during a firefighting operation. Controls should include prevention measures such as bunding and drainage to a place where contamination will not reach drinking water supplies or enter rivers and streams.

Sources

Love Canal

Beck E C. The Love Canal tragedy. *Environmental Protection Agency Journal*, January 1979. www.epa.gov/history/topics/lovecanal/01.htm

US Environmental Protection Agency. Love Canal documents and resources. www.epa.gov/history/topics/lovecanal

Seveso

Control of Major Accident Hazards Regulations 1999, amended 2005

Health and Safety Executive. Control of major accident hazards. www.hse.gov.uk/comah

Health and Safety Executive. Icmesa chemical company, Seveso, Italy, 10 July 1976. www.hse.gov.uk/comah/sragtech/caseseveso76.htm

Sandoz

1986: Chemical spill turns Rhine red. BBC News Online: On this day, 1 November. http://news.bbc.co.uk/onthisday/hi/dates/stories/november/1/newsid_4679000/4679789.stm

Chapter 8: Unwelcome off-site consequences

It is bad enough when a serious incident occurs that is successfully contained within the factory perimeter, but fires and explosions have an unwelcome habit of failing to recognise boundaries. Even when no one off site is hurt, great fear can be aroused among the local population and the press will have a field day. Company reputations may not be destroyed but they can be severely dented locally by these events.

The explosion and fire at Chemstar Limited, Manchester, England, 1981

While the incident in 1981 at a small chemical works that processed waste chemical materials in Stalybridge near Manchester does not rank in severity with the major disasters I have described elsewhere, the incident conveys some lessons worth studying here.

What happened?

Chemstar Ltd processed and recovered waste chemical materials of many kinds. Half an hour before midnight on 6 September 1981, an explosion occurred at the works followed by a raging fire that spread throughout the site, propelling drums of blazing solvents off site in a series of further explosions.

Why?

A pot still was being used to distil 6,000 litres of hexane in order to remove contaminants. The main water supply to the factory had been cut off when the local reservoir was drained and a temporary supply was being taken from a nearby stream to feed the still's steam condenser.

That night the supply of water to the condenser was interrupted and highly flammable hexane vapour began to fill the distillation room.

What happened next?

An employee noticed a strong smell and, together with a delivery truck driver visiting the site, went to the distillation room to investigate. At that moment the vapour was ignited, probably by an oil fired boiler, and blew up the building. The truck driver was killed in the explosion and the employee suffered serious burns. The blast shook buildings in Stalybridge and more than 1,000 people had to be evacuated from their homes as the many drums of flammable solvents stored on site exploded throughout the night.

As the drums exploded, some were thrown from the site, with one reported to have hit the roof of a house half a mile away. It took two days, 37 fire appliances and 200 firemen to bring the blaze under control.

Lessons
Although the surrounding land and the River Tame were contaminated by
traces of the many different chemicals that had been stored at Chemstar,
fortunately this event did not have the major health and environmental
consequences of, say, the Love Canal, Seveso or Sandoz disasters. But it
was a wake-up call to safety professionals in the UK that even small
chemical works can present risks that, if not properly managed, will pose
serious threats to local communities when processes go wrong. It takes a
long time to remove contamination. The site of the destroyed factory was
finally cleaned up in 1989.

The operator had been trained in continuous distillation methods but was
unfamiliar with batch processing and the correct control valve settings for
normal and emergency operation.

Maintaining a reliable supply of water to the condenser was critical to the
safety of the operation. This was not the first time that the temporary
water supply to the condenser, which was essential for the safe distillation
of flammable liquids, had failed. When this had happened before, it had
been noticed that vapours had been given off, but the risk of an explosion
had been ignored.

The condenser's discharge vent was inside the building, allowing vapour to
gather there and find a source of ignition; it should have been vented
safely to a collector outside.

The chemical release and fire at Associated Octel Company Limited, Ellesmere Port, England, 1994
A potentially much more serious event occurred a few years later at the
factory of the Associated Octel Company Ltd in Ellesmere Port, Cheshire,
where tetraethyl lead, an antiknock additive to petrol, was being made.

What happened?
At about 8.30 in the morning of 1 February 1994, a recirculating pump at
a reactor vessel began to leak a toxic, corrosive and highly flammable
solution consisting mainly of ethyl chloride, a flammable liquefied gas,
mixed with hydrogen chloride, a toxic and corrosive gas, and a catalyst,
aluminium chloride. The reactor vessel had a capacity of 25 tonnes.

Why?
Investigation found that it was likely that a flange securing the pump to
pipework had corroded and worked loose, allowing liquid that should
have been recirculated to escape, though it was also possible that a plastic
bellows connecting the pump discharge to the pipework had failed.

The aftermath of the chemical leak and fire at Associated Octel, 1 February 1994.
David Eves

What happened next?
As leakage of the reactor's contents continued a dense cloud of white vapour formed, spreading throughout the works until it rolled away off site, towards Ellesmere Port and Merseyside. Attempts to stop this by isolating the leak were hampered for a while by difficulty in reaching and operating manual isolation valves.

In the meantime a pool of liquid had begun to collect around the base of the reactor, giving off flammable ethyl chloride vapour. Some 90 minutes after the leakage had begun the pool burst into flame, with the vapours probably ignited by a nearby compressor.

Both the company's and the local authority's emergency services responded rapidly, following their emergency plans for chemical accidents, but before the fire could be brought under control and the escape stopped, other pipework and flanges were damaged. Fires broke out elsewhere on the plant; an explosion could have damaged a nearby chlorine storage installation. Had this become involved the off-site consequences could have been very severe. Fortunately, though not without difficulty, the fires were brought under control and the factory – and Merseyside – saved.

An investigation by the HSE followed, the company was prosecuted for failure to maintain the plant safely and was fined £150,000.

Lessons

As usual, one thing led to another. A relatively minor corrosion or failure of pipework on a critical section of the plant followed by failure to isolate the leak quickly allowed a large spillage of toxic, corrosive and flammable materials to occur. This led unnecessarily to a major fire which threatened to involve hazardous materials in other parts of the factory and cause an off-site catastrophe.

The manual control valves essential to isolating the leaking pump were hard to reach and operate in an emergency that involved hazardous materials. Remote control shut off valves (ROSOVs) should have been installed.

The use of flexible bellows in pipework carrying hazardous materials was not good practice. Remember Flixborough.

In spite of the high hazards on this site, a formal system had not been established for reporting faults such as corrosion of flanges and for maintaining the equipment involved in this chemical release, which could have had very severe off-site consequences.

The fire at Allied Colloids, Bradford, England, 1992

The Sandoz fire and pollution incident described in Chapter 7 might seem unusual, but a rather similar event occurred a few years later at a warehouse in Bradford, West Yorkshire.

The fire at Allied Colloids in Bradford, 21 July 1992.
David Eves

What happened?

On 21 July 1992 a fire broke out at a raw materials warehouse on the Allied Colloids site at Low Moor. Within the warehouse, two rooms had been allocated for the storage of oxidising and flammable materials. One of these rooms had a blown air steam heating system as it had originally been designed to store products needing protection from frost.

Why?

That morning the steam heated blowers were turned on to dry out moisture, their steam line inadvertently heating several kegs of AZDN (azobisisobutyronitrile, a chemical mainly used in polymerisation reactions) stacked nearby. A number of similar kegs and others containing an oxidizing chemical were stored in the same room.

The heated kegs burst, spilling their powdery contents onto the floor. The alarm was raised by an employee who thought that the fine powder still hovering in the atmosphere was smoke, but it was decided that it presented no danger and could be cleaned up later.

The worker then noticed smoke or vapour coming from a sack of sodium persulphate (SPS) beneath the kegs and heard a hissing sound. As he was going for water to damp it down it suddenly burst into flame, which rapidly flashed around the room. Soon the entire building was on fire, with smoke spreading across the nearby motorway.

What happened next?

The fire brigade successfully brought the blaze under control within a day but stood by for another 18 days in case any hazardous materials reignited. In the meantime there had been considerable environmental pollution caused by the runoff of water used to control the fire into the nearby rivers, the Aire and the Calder.

Lessons

It was a mistake to have stored AZDN in the same room as an oxidising substance, SPS. There had been a mix-up in the documentation.

Once again, firewater had been allowed to run off-site and cause environmental pollution.

The fire at Albright and Wilson Limited, Avonmouth, England, 1996

Although the fire that occurred at Avonmouth on 3 October 1996 was also not a major disaster, useful lessons can be drawn from the experience.

The aftermath of the explosion at Albright and Wilson in Avonmouth, 3 October 1996.
Paul Glendell/ www.glendell.co.uk

What happened?

A road tanker arrived at Albright and Wilson's Avonmouth chemical works at about 10.30 that morning to deliver a load of epichlorohydrin that had been ordered and was expected. Not long after offloading into a dedicated epichlorohydrin storage tank had begun, several explosions followed and then a fire broke out.

Why?

The paperwork accompanying the load was not checked by Albright and Wilson's staff before offloading was allowed to begin. If they had examined the documentation they would have discovered that the tanker had mistakenly brought them a load of sodium chlorite, which reacts explosively with epichlorohydrin. The haulage contractor phoned to advise the firm as it spotted the error that morning, but was too late to prevent the offloading.

What happened next?

As the fire developed, a vast plume of black smoke containing toxic hydrogen chloride spread over the M5 and M4 motorways, the Severn Bridge and the railway. These all had to be closed, causing major traffic disruption. Fortunately, there were no more serious consequences and the fire was brought under control. The HSE investigated and Albright and Wilson were subsequently prosecuted and fined £60,000.

Lessons

It is essential to check that a load of hazardous material coming from elsewhere is actually what it purports to be. The receiver failed to do this, although the documentation carried by the haulage contractor's driver would have revealed the error. Nor had the tanker's hazard markings been checked, which might have alerted staff to the danger.

No system had been put in place to prevent inadvertent mixing of materials that might react dangerously with each other.

Sources

Chemstar

Health and Safety Executive. *Explosion and fire at Chemstar Ltd, 6 September 1981.* Sudbury: HSE Books, 1982

Health and Safety Executive. The explosion and fire at Chemstar Limited, 6th September 1981. www.hse.gov.uk/COMAH/sragtech/casechemstar81.htm

Associated Octel

Health and Safety Executive. *The chemical release and fire at the Associated Octel Company Limited: A report of the investigation by the Health and Safety Executive into the chemical release and fire at the Associated Octel Company, Ellesmere Port on 1 and 2 February 1994.* Sudbury: HSE Books, 1996

Health and Safety Executive. The chemical release and fire at the Associated Octel Company Limited, Ellesmere Port, Cheshire. 1st February 1994. www.hse.gov.uk/comah/sragtech/caseoctel94.htm

Allied Colloids

Health and Safety Executive. *Fire at Allied Colloids Ltd.* Sudbury: HSE Books, 1994

Health and Safety Executive. The fire at Allied Colloids Limited, Low Moor, Bradford, 21st July 1992. www.hse.gov.uk/COMAH/sragtech/casealliedcol92.htm

Albright and Wilson

Health and Safety Executive. The fire at Albright and Wilson, Avonmouth, 3 October 1996. www.hse.gov.uk/comah/sragtech/casealbright96.htm

Chapter 9: High explosives

Remember, remember the fifth of November, / Gunpowder, treason and plot
(Traditional)

Explosives have been manufactured for hundreds of years in the pursuit of warfare and for peaceful industrial applications such as mining and demolition. As our Chief Inspector of Explosives once said to me, "One moment it's there, the next moment it isn't." Large numbers of workers have tragically been killed in the many industrial disasters associated with explosives.

But, looking on the positive side, these awful experiences led to a way being found to regulate the very high risks involved in the manufacture and storage of these chemicals and drove the industry to pursue a stronger safety culture, as we shall see.

Leiden, The Netherlands, 1807

A century and a half after a disastrous gunpowder explosion had destroyed the centre of the Dutch city of Delft, a ship laden with black powder blew up in the centre of Leiden, killing 151 people, 50 of them schoolchildren, and injuring 2,000. Hundreds of houses were demolished.

The Netherlands were ruled at the time by a brother of Napoleon Bonaparte, the French Emperor. Napoleon decreed that in future a licence from the state would be required to manufacture or store explosives, with facilities separated into three levels of risk:

- those facilities too dangerous to be allowed inside a city
- facilities that could be allowed inside a city if their safety could be demonstrated by the owner
- facilities that could always be allowed.

The language used by Napoleon to describe these risks may have been different but the concepts resemble the thinking of the HSE nearly 200 years later in *The tolerability of risk from nuclear power stations*, a publication that attempted to distinguish between 'acceptable', 'tolerable' and 'unacceptable' risks.

Following the decree, any arguments over safety were thus no longer disputes between the operator and Dutch citizens living in the neighbourhoods of hazardous premises, but now also involved the state as arbiter. The licensing requirement was absorbed into Dutch factory safety

Louis Bonaparte, then King of Holland, inspects the damage caused by the explosion of a powder ship at Leiden, 12 January 1807.
Painting by Carel Lodewijk Hansen

law in 1875, the same year that the Explosives Act introduced licensing of explosive factories in the UK.

Meanwhile, in the USA...

The DuPont powder mill explosion, Delaware, 1857

A devastating explosion near Wilmington, Delaware, in 1857 led to a family firm's determined campaign over the next 150 years to raise safety in their company to its highest attainable level.

What happened?
Eleutherian Mills, DuPont's iconic gunpowder factory on the banks of the Brandywine Creek at Wilmington, blew up on 22 August 1857.

One of the du Pont family, Alexis, was being helped by seven of his workmen to move a heavy bin from a building that had been used as a black powder store since 1812. As they struggled with it the metal bin struck the wall, sparking a small explosion which engulfed them in fire. Badly burnt and with their clothes alight, they retreated to save themselves. Alexis du Pont is even said to have jumped into the creek. Once he had dowsed himself he went back to the building to see if any fires were still burning that could endanger the rest of the works. But as he approached it the entire building was suddenly blown asunder.

Alexis was found among the ruins, seriously maimed but still alive. He is said to have calmly given instructions to the survivors to extinguish any remaining flames and protect the rest of the factory. He died from his injuries some hours later, but not before saying goodbye to his workmates. Three of the men helping him also died; the others survived, though with terrible burns.

Why?
In spite of frequent cleaning of the store, over the years black powder had been unwittingly allowed to slip beneath the floorboards. Once the building caught fire, a massive explosion was inevitable.

What happened next?
The 1857 explosion was by no means the first to take lives at the powder mill and sadly it would not be the last, but the family was determined to achieve the highest possible safety standards in their dangerous business. Legend has it that the seriousness of their intent was demonstrated by an unusual practice: a du Pont would always live on site, showing confidence in the company's management of risks.

Lessons
There was another catastrophic event in 1863 when 40 men were killed. There were no legal requirements in those days to guide the company, but things did get better, slowly but surely, as they gradually established standards and adopted safety improvements. These included allowing no nails in the soles of footwear, to avoid the risk of a spark igniting powder, establishing separation distances to prevent the effects of a blast at one building damaging others, and designing buildings so that in the event of an explosion the blast would be directed across the creek and away from the mill.

It is only fair to say that through its unswerving pursuit of safety for over a century and a half since 1857, DuPont has become one of the best-performing companies in the world today from a safety perspective, aiming at zero injuries and with its accident frequency rates usually a tenth of the chemical industry's average.

But even the best can still make mistakes. In 2002 an explosion at a DuPont company's chemical works in Mississippi propelled debris into a neighbouring refinery, attracting investigations by the safety authorities. However, in spite of this setback, the company's attitude towards safety remains very impressive. I have known a now-retired chairman of DuPont UK for many years. He would always ask his driver to check the equipment in the boot before setting off anywhere and he would never carry bags in both hands downstairs: the company rule was always to keep one hand for yourself.

I once had the pleasure of being asked to give some awards to companies for health and safety achievements on behalf of the Engineering Employers' Federation. There was a photographer there to record it all for posterity. Du Pont had won an award and they brought along quite a big party to receive it. To do them justice the photographer wanted the back row to stand on some chairs so they could be seen. They politely refused, explaining that this would be in breach of their company's safety rules.

Even small demonstrations of a positive attitude towards safety are revealing. Leadership is about example. Little things do mean a lot.

Silvertown, London, 1917

Londoners had become used to bombing raids by Zeppelins during the First World War, but none of these would cause as much death and damage in a single event as a massive explosion that occurred in 1917 at a munitions factory by the River Thames in east London.

What happened?

To help the war effort the dangerous process of manufacturing trinitrotoluene (TNT) had unwisely been established at an existing, disused chemical works in the highly populated area of Silvertown, east London.

On 19 January 1917 at about seven in the evening 73 people were killed and more than 400 injured when 50 tons of TNT exploded at the Brunner Mond factory. Had the explosion occurred earlier in the day many more workers would have been present and the death toll would have been far greater.

Why?

The explosion had been triggered by a small fire in the factory as attempts were being made to put it out. The enormous blast completely destroyed the factory, together with railway trucks containing TNT and a nearby gasholder.

What happened next?

The thunderclap rattled the whole of London, shattering windows and shaking buildings, and was said to have been heard 100 miles away. Hundreds of homes and warehouses were damaged, many even destroyed in neighbouring streets.

Although this was wartime, the government had to act quickly to allay the public's alarm about what had happened. An inquiry was led by Sir Ernley Blackwell. He ruled out an enemy raid as a possible cause, but criticised the inappropriate location of the plant and poor safety management at the

Houses destroyed by the explosion of the Brunner Mond factory in Silvertown, 19 January 1917. *Newham Archives and Local Studies Library*

factory which he believed had contributed to the scale of the disaster. There were factories elsewhere in the country where TNT was being made under safer conditions than at Silvertown. But before the Great War ended, another explosives factory blew up in Nottingham, killing 134 people.

Lessons

The Explosives Act of 1875 had set standards for the safe manufacture of explosives and this legislation was sufficiently effective in peacetime to remain on the statute book until the end of the 20th century. Mixing of high explosives is normally safe when done under controlled conditions, in carefully segregated buildings at isolated locations. And mixing of TNT famously requires the operator to sit on a one-legged stool, so that if he falls asleep on the job, he is jolted awake!

Sources

Leiden
Dutch Wikipedia page on the explosion: http://nl.wikipedia.org/wiki/Leidse_buskruitramp (in Dutch)
Reitsma H J. The explosion of a ship, loaded with black powder, in Leiden in 1807. *International Journal of Impact Engineering* May 2001; 25 (5): 507–514

DuPont, Eleutherian Mills
DuPont website. www2.dupont.com
The Center for Land Use Interpretation. Sublime explosive pastoral: a visit to DuPont on the Brandywine. *The Lay of the Land* Spring 2005; 28. www.clui.org/clui_4_1/lotl/v28/k.html

Silvertown
Explosives Act 1875
Hill G and Bloch H. *The Silvertown Explosion: London 1917*. Stroud: Tempus Publishing, 2003
London's biggest explosion. www.portcities.org.uk/london/server/show/ConNarrative.60/Londons-biggest-explosion.html

General
US Chemical Safety and Hazard Investigation Board. www.csb.gov

Chapter 10: Maritime disasters

Phlebas the Phoenician, a fortnight dead,
Forgot the cry of gulls, and the deep sea swell,
And the profit and the loss
(From *The Waste Land: Death by Water* by T S Eliot, 1888–1965)

Drawing of the
Princess Alice
collision, 3 September
1878.
Harper's Weekly,
12 October 1878

The sinking of the *Princess Alice*, River Thames, London, 1878

By the late 19th century, the Port of London was becoming increasingly busy. Hundreds of vessels, from large liners to tugs, barges and lighters, used the River Thames each day. Despite ever larger and faster ships, there were no precise 'rules of the road'. Confusion inevitably led to tragedy.

In 1878 the paddle steamer *Princess Alice* sank after a needless collision with the *Bywell Castle*, a collier, in Galleons Reach. More than 600 people lost their lives in what is still the worst ever disaster on a British waterway. As they struggled in the filthy water many were gassed even before they drowned by noxious fumes given off from the river, which was then an open sewer.

An inquiry followed the tragedy and the rules for ships using the river were tightened up somewhat. But history repeated itself a century later, as we shall find. In the meantime an even greater disaster occurred off the coast of Newfoundland.

The loss of the *Titanic*, North Atlantic, 1912

The loss of the White Star Line's 'unsinkable' transatlantic liner *Titanic* on its maiden voyage to the USA in 1912, the epic subject of a hugely successful Hollywood movie, is a disaster that everyone must have heard about. I mention it here because understanding its causes and the consequences are still very relevant to avoiding disasters today.

What happened?

The 46,000-ton ocean liner was a giant in its time, designed with extreme comfort, speed and safety in mind. With 16 separate watertight compartments, it was believed to be unsinkable, since if one or two compartments were penetrated and flooded the others were more than sufficient to keep the ship afloat. Or so it was thought.

Just before midnight on 14 April 1912, nearing the end of its highly publicised transatlantic voyage, the ship was sailing at speed south of the Grand Banks when it struck an iceberg. Within three hours, with more than 2,200 passengers and crew on board, the *Titanic* had sunk.

Why?

It was known that icebergs were drifting further south than usual that year but it is thought that the captain ignored warnings, feeling under

Survivors of the *Titanic* disaster are rescued by the *Carpathia*, 15 April 1912.
US National Archives

pressure from the owners to record a fast maiden crossing by the most direct route. When the ship's lookout saw the fatal iceberg looming out of the dark and warned the helmsman, it was already too late to avoid it.

Although the *Titanic* was believed to be unsinkable because of its design, striking the iceberg a glancing blow at speed was sufficient to hole six of the ship's watertight compartments.

What happened next?

As these flooded, the ship began to list, making it impossible to launch some of the lifeboats. In any case far too few were carried for the numbers of people aboard. Before passing ships arrived to pick up survivors, the ship had sunk and 1,571 people had drowned in the freezing waters.

There might have been more survivors had the radio operator of a nearby ship, the *Californian*, not been off duty. The *Californian* remained unaware of the *Titanic*'s plight and steamed on.

Lessons

As a result of investigations and recommendations many changes were made to ship design and management and new international laws were introduced to protect the Safety of Life at Sea (SOLAS). In future, ships would be required to maintain a continuous radio watch, provide sufficient lifeboat spaces for every person on board and carry out lifeboat drills. An international ice patrol was introduced to ensure early warnings of icebergs.

The mysterious sinking of MV *Derbyshire*, South China Sea, 1980

The bulk carrier MV *Derbyshire* is the biggest British-registered merchant ship ever to have been lost at sea. Its story is revealing about our investigation and inquiry processes.

What happened?

The *Derbyshire* disappeared in the South China Sea during an intense tropical storm, Typhoon Orchid, on 9 or 10 September 1980 while on her way from Canada to Japan. The 44 people who were on board went down with her.

Why?

Bulk carriers had a poor record, with about 17 being lost every year. However, the loss of the *Derbyshire* was unexpected: the ship was only four years old, the master and crew were very experienced, she was British-built and classified A1 at Lloyds.

Arguments raged about the cause of her sinking for the next 20 years. The position of the storm meant that the ship had been unable to change course safely to avoid the hurricane-force winds. Speculation about the wave height she might have encountered ranged from 10 to even 30 metres, and it was suggested that the waves were longer than the ship, submerging her bows and preventing her from rising above them.

What happened next?

The government resisted holding a formal investigation into the loss of the *Derbyshire*, arguing that in the absence of any evidence an inquiry would be futile. This decision prompted the victims' families to form an association and fight for years for the truth. They eventually succeeded in their demands for a proper inquiry.

Subsequent events added weight to their case. In March 1982 a sister ship, the *Tyne Bridge*, ran into heavy weather in the North Sea, which caused cracks in her deck forward of the bridge. Four other sister ships were then found to have damage in the same area of decking. Evidence emerged that the *Derbyshire* had also experienced this problem, which centred around frame 65, part of these ships' common structure.

Data about frame 65 was collected by a ship surveyor, who was the father of the fourth engineer on the *Derbyshire*, and sent to the Department of Transport (DoT) in September 1982 and again in June 1983. He received no immediate reply but in July 1985 the DoT issued a draft report that suggested that the *Derbyshire* might have been lost due to damage in front of the bridge in the region of frame 65. In March 1986 the report was finally published, but it now said that the loss of the ship could have been due to various other reasons.

A tipping point in the investigations came when another sister ship, the *Kowloon Bridge*, ran aground off the coast of Ireland after suffering severe cracking of the deck in heavy weather in the North Atlantic. Shortly after grounding she broke her back in the vicinity of frame 65. Faced with this, the government at last agreed to hold an inquiry into the loss of the *Derbyshire*. This took place in 1987 and found that:

> For the reasons stated in this Report the Court finds that the *Derbyshire* was probably overwhelmed by the forces of nature in typhoon Orchid, possibly after getting beam on to wind and sea, off Okinawa in darkness on the night of 9/10 September 1980 with the loss of 44 lives. The evidence available does not support any firmer conclusion.

Naturally, the families were outraged, believing that the evidence of the *Kowloon Bridge* had been deliberately ignored. Still convinced that frame 65 had something to do with the loss of the *Derbyshire*, they demanded an underwater survey.

Their persistence succeeded, although it did not confirm their suspicion. An expedition to the sunken ship took place in 1997 and 1998. The surveyors found that it was not frame 65 that had failed. Instead they concluded that a hatch on the foredeck had failed because it had not been properly secured, allowing water to flood progressively into the forward compartments, making it inevitable that the ship would sink in such heavy seas. It seemed to point towards negligence by the crew to secure the hatch.

However, this was not the end of the sad saga. A new government decided to reopen the inquiry and a number of experts gave evidence in the spring of 2000. The inquiry finally decided that the sinking had been due to the damage caused by heavy seas to air pipes mounted on the fore deck allowing water to begin flooding the forward compartment, exposing the fore hatch to severe pounding until it eventually failed. The crew were exonerated.

Lessons
Seventeen bulk carriers were being lost at sea every year during the 1980s. Prompted by the sinking of the *Derbyshire* and thanks to improvements in design and construction of this kind of large cargo vessel, few are now being lost.

Governments, regulators and investigators underestimate at their peril the need for families of the victims of disaster to seek justice and closure, their ability to bond together and fight endlessly for the truth. Time and right are often on their side.

The *Marchioness* disaster, River Thames, London, 1989
These days there can be few more pleasurable prospects than cruising on the River Thames with friends during a summer evening. But on 20 August 1989 a happy occasion for 132 young people enjoying a private birthday party on the pleasure craft *Marchioness* was to turn into tragedy.

What happened?
Fifty-one of the partygoers on board the *Marchioness* drowned in the Thames that night when their boat was struck and mounted by a much larger vessel, the *Bowbelle*, near Blackfriars Bridge. The *Marchioness* capsized and sank in about half a minute. There were no rescue boats in

The wreck of the
Marchioness is raised
from the Thames,
August 1989.
Getty Images

the immediate vicinity. Most of the survivors were on the upper deck;
many of the victims were down below. Twenty-four bodies were later
recovered from the wreckage.

Why?
The master and crew of the *Bowbelle* had not been keeping a proper
lookout and did not see the smaller craft they were bearing down on. Nor
did the captain of the *Marchioness* see the *Bowbelle* coming up behind.

What happened next?
The collision was investigated by the Marine Accident Investigation
Branch of the Department of Transport. Their findings were that:

- both vessels had poor visibility from their wheelhouses
- both vessels were in the centre of the river
- the lookout at the bow of the *Bowbelle* was unclear about his
  instructions.

Later, Captain Henderson, the master of the *Bowbelle*, was tried and acquitted
on a charge of failing to keep a proper lookout. Even so, a Coroner's inquest
held in 1995 found that the victims had been unlawfully killed.

John Prescott MP, later to become Deputy Prime Minister but then the
shadow Transport Minister, came to see the HSE in the early 1990s. He told

us that he was pressing for a public inquiry into what had become known as the Marchioness Disaster, and that he intended to transfer responsibility for regulating marine safety from the Department of Transport to the HSE when a Labour government was next elected. However, that was not to happen; by the time his party came to power in 1997 responsibilities had already been given by the previous government to a newly formed Maritime and Coastguard Agency.

Lessons

At first the families' demand for a public inquiry fell on deaf ears, but an action group was formed and began to campaign vigorously. True to a promise made to the families, in 2000 the Deputy Prime Minister ordered a public inquiry into the circumstances of the collision to be held under Lord Justice Clarke. His report blamed poor lookouts on both vessels for the collision and criticised the owners and managers of both vessels for failing to properly instruct and monitor their crews. Not keeping a proper lookout is to invite disaster.

Attention was also drawn to the design of multidecked pleasure boats, in particular the need to escape rapidly from lower decks (most of the survivors were on the upper deck). It was also pointed out that busy waterways, where there is a day and night risk of collision, need a dedicated search and rescue service.

Following recommendations to improve river safety, the government asked the Maritime and Coastguard Agency, the Port of London Authority and the Royal National Lifeboat Institution (RNLI) to work together to set up a dedicated search and rescue service for the tidal River Thames. As a result the RNLI established lifeboat stations on the Thames at Tower Pier, Chiswick Pier, Teddington and Gravesend in 2002.

The capsizing of the *Herald of Free Enterprise*, Zeebrugge, Belgium, 1987

The MS *Herald of Free Enterprise* was a large, modern roll-on, roll-off ferry, one of three sister ships owned and operated by Townsend Thoresen that plied the cross-Channel routes from Dover to French and Belgian ports. On the evening of 6 March 1987 it was setting off to return from Zeebrugge when disaster struck.

What happened?

As the ferry moved out of harbour into the open sea, picking up speed, it scooped in water through the bow door opening, listed and in less than a minute had capsized onto its side, resting in shallow water on sand not far from the shore. Many of those on board were rescued by the Belgian

Navy but 193 passengers and crew lost their lives in the worst postwar disaster to have happened to a British ship.

Why?

Ro-ro ferries are designed with speed and efficiency of loading in mind and allow vehicles to drive on one end and off the other through large openings at the bows and stern that give access to several car decks. These decks are clear from stem to stern without intervening watertight compartments; watertight doors fitted to the bow opening should be closed after loading and before putting to sea. The *Herald* had left port with the bow doors open.

What happened next?

Investigation revealed that the bow doors could not be seen from the bridge. The officers had no technical means of knowing that they had been closed, such as a bell or warning light. They wrongly assumed that the doors had been closed; in fact the assistant bosun whose responsibility it was to check this was asleep in his cabin. The first officer who would normally be on deck during the operation, conscious of the need to leave on schedule, had returned to the wheelhouse before the ship set off and was unaware that no one was checking the closing of the doors. Crew members did not think to do this as it was not their responsibility.

A public inquiry was held in July 1987 under Mr Justice Sheen, whose report severely criticised Townsend Thoresen, now part of the P&O Group.

The capsized *Herald of Free Enterprise* off Zeebrugge.
AFP/Getty Images

He found that the capsize had been the joint fault of the master, the chief officer, the assistant bosun and Townsend Thoresen, and identified "a disease of sloppiness" and negligence at every level of the company.

A coroner's inquest recorded a jury verdict of 'unlawful killing'. The assistant bosun was the only person to accept any responsibility; a corporate manslaughter case against the company failed, leading to demands for a strengthening of the law. But it would be 2007 before Parliament passed the Corporate Manslaughter and Corporate Homicide Bill.

Lessons

The root cause of the disaster was a poor corporate safety culture that led that night to a complete failure to manage a system that relied on human factors. The officers and crew failed to adhere to a procedure that would have ensured the doors were closed before leaving port. Commercial pressures on the crew to achieve a quick turn around were also in play and the system took no account of the possibility of human error. Safety was not at the forefront of their minds.

Technical improvements in the design and management of ro-ro ferries were made in the light of this tragic experience, including fitting indicators on the bridge to report the status of the watertight doors and watertight ramps at the bows, and new requirements were introduced by the International Maritime Organisation to prohibit the construction of new ships with open decks the length of the car decks on the *Herald*.

However, these improvements would not prevent an even worse ferry disaster in 1994.

The sinking of the *Estonia*, Baltic Sea, 1994

On the night of 28 September 1994, the ferry *Estonia* was carrying almost a thousand passengers and crew across the Baltic from Tallinn to Stockholm. The sea conditions were rough, though not excessively so.

What happened?

During the night heavy seas damaged the ship, flooding the car deck until, destabilised, the vessel listed and sank. 852 people lost their lives.

Why?

The design of the ship's bows protected it from taking on water from heavy seas into the car deck by the provision of a metal 'bow visor' protecting the ramp closing the car deck. During the night the visor, battered by the storm, was carried away, exposing the car deck ramp, which was not strong enough to withstand the onslaught.

What happened next?

The ramp also failed and as it took on more water the ship began to list very badly, preventing lifeboats from being launched. A mayday signal was sent but as the ship listed further it became impossible for those below deck to escape from the canting lower decks. Only those passengers and crew who had managed to get on deck and hang on until help arrived were saved before the vessel foundered.

Lessons

This terrible disaster led to further important changes in safety regulations and the design of ferries, including new standards for life rafts that could be launched in the event of lifeboats being disabled, provision of distress beacons, and a new code of conduct for ships that were operating in the busy Baltic Sea.

Not everyone marches to the sound of the same drum. On 26 September 2002 an overloaded Senegalese ferry, *Le Joola*, capsized off the coast of the Gambia with the loss of about 2,000 lives. Its legal capacity was 280. There are frequent reports of ferry disasters in the Philippines: the worst ever loss of life in a civilian marine accident occurred when the *Doña Paz* sank in 1987. Over 4,000 people drowned.

Sources

Princess Alice
Vincent W T. The Princess Alice disaster. In: *The records of the Woolwich district*. London: J S Virtue & Co., 1888–1890. www.yellins.com/woolwichferry/thames/PrincessAlice.htm

Titanic
Titanic Historical Society. www.titanichistoricalsociety.org
Titanic Inquiry Project. www.titanicinquiry.org

Derbyshire
Department for Transport. MV Derbyshire surveys: UK/EC assessors' report: a summary. www.dft.gov.uk/pgr/shippingports/shipping/safety/mvderbyshire/
mvderbyshiresurveysukecasses5012
Merseyside Maritime Museum. The sinking of MV Derbyshire. www.liverpoolmuseums.org.uk/maritime/exhibitions/derbyshire

Marchioness
1989: Marchioness river crash 'kills 30'. BBC News Online: On this day, 20 August. http://news.bbc.co.uk/onthisday/hi/dates/stories/august/20/newsid_2500000/2500211.stm
Clarke, Lord Justice. *Thames safety inquiry*. London: Stationery Office Books, 1999

Herald of Free Enterprise
Department of Transport. *MV Herald of Free Enterprise. Report of Court No. 8074: formal investigation.* London: HMSO, 1987
Marine Accident Investigation Branch. *Herald of Free Enterprise report.* www.maib.gov.uk/publications/investigation_reports/herald_of_free_enterprise/herald_of_free_enterprise_report.cfm

Estonia
Estonian, Finnish and Swedish Governments. *Final report on the capsizing on 28 September 1994 in the Baltic Sea of the ro-ro passenger vessel MV Estonia.* Helsinki: The Joint Accident Investigation Committee of MV Estonia, 1997. www.onnettomuustutkinta.fi/estonia

General
International Maritime Organization. www.imo.org
Maritime and Coastguard Agency. www.mcga.gov.uk

Chapter 11 – Marine pollution

Most of the worst environmental disasters have been caused by oil tankers, sometimes as a result of a mistake by the officers on board.

Torrey Canyon, Cornwall, England, 1967

The world's first major spillage of oil occurred when the *Torrey Canyon* was wrecked off the western coast of Cornwall in March 1967. At the time, such an environmental catastrophe was almost unimaginable. That naïve belief was to change as the extraordinary peacetime scenes of a ship being bombed by the RAF were brought into living rooms by television news. It was but the first of many super tanker pollution disasters.

What happened?

On 18 March 1967 the *Torrey Canyon* was sailing for Milford Haven, Pembrokeshire, where its cargo of 80,000 tonnes of crude oil was to be discharged.

Why?

As the supertanker passed between the Isles of Scilly and the mainland, she was approaching some fishing vessels. Trying to avoid colliding with these, the skipper and the helmsman (actually the cook) were – almost unbelievably – unsure whether they were steering the ship manually or by autopilot, and of quite where they were: the ship's charts for the area were

Oil from the *Torrey Canyon* is set on fire in an attempt to disperse it, March 1967.
Time & Life Pictures/ Getty Images

small-scale and its navigational system was far from state of the art. While all this was being sorted out she ran onto the Seven Stones rocks, where she remained stranded.

What happened next?
As an ever-widening oil slick began to drift towards Brittany and Cornwall, help arrived in the form of a Dutch salvage team. Sadly a member of the team was killed as they made unsuccessful attempts to float the ship off. The ship finally broke apart after remaining stranded for several days and being bombed by aircraft in an eventually successful attempt to sink her.

By then the oil slick (estimated at 270 square miles) had spread along 50 miles of the French coastline and 120 miles of Cornish coast, causing great environmental and ecological damage and severely harming the local economies.

Lessons
Human factors clearly played a big part in initiating this disaster, whose effects were then exacerbated by technical problems and the absence of an effective emergency plan.

It was found that foam booms used in an attempt to contain the oil were too fragile to be effective in severe sea conditions, and that using toxic detergents to break up the oil slick caused more damage by emulsifying the oil.

The *Amoco Cadiz* founders off the coast of Brittany, 16 March 1978.
National Oceanic and Atmospheric Administration

The *Torrey Canyon* disaster led to a tightening of international law, imposing strict liability on ship owners without the need to prove negligence, and the 1973 International Convention for the Prevention of Pollution from Ships. But we were soon to discover that these changes, though welcome, would not prevent even worse disasters.

Amoco Cadiz, Brittany, France, 1978

A record for the largest oil spill from a tanker – since surpassed several times – was set on 16 March 1978 when the supertanker *Amoco Cadiz*, carrying 1.6 million barrels of oil, ran onto rocks three miles off the coast of Brittany.

What happened and why?
Nearing the end of its voyage from the Persian Gulf to the Netherlands, as it approached the English Channel in the early morning heading for Lyme Bay, the *Amoco Cadiz* ran into heavy weather. As the wind rose and conditions worsened, the ship's rudder was struck and damaged by heavy seas and it could no longer be steered. At 10.20 the vessel reported that it was no longer manoeuvrable and at 11.00 a call was made for tugs to assist her.

What happened next?
A German tug responded and arrived soon after midday, but attempts to secure a towline proved difficult in the stormy conditions, and several tow lines broke as the huge ship drifted with the wind towards the French coast. It was almost nine o'clock in the evening before it was secured, but almost immediately after that it grounded on the sea bottom, flooding the engine compartment. Half an hour later its hull split open and began spilling oil as it grounded again in the heavy seas. Its crew was safely rescued by helicopter but by the following morning the ship had broken in two, shedding its entire cargo.

A long oil slick was now spreading 45 miles along the sandy tourist beaches of Brittany. A clean-up operation proved difficult because of emulsification of the oil and a number of Brittany's characteristic rocky coves remained contaminated for some years. Inevitably, the local wildlife and fishing industry suffered severely and holiday resorts lost visitor numbers.

The disaster is said to have cost these industries $250 million. The French government claimed $2 billion in the US courts but eventually settled for $120 million from Amoco in 1990.

Exxon Valdez, Alaska, 1989

While the oil spills off the French and British coasts were bad enough, an environmental disaster that surpassed these by far was to occur in one of the world's largely unspoilt wildernesses, Alaska.

What happened?
On 24 March 1989 at around 11 pm, an oil tanker, the *Exxon Valdez*, was sailing out of Prince William Sound towards the open sea when, with permission from the US Coast Guard, it left the normal shipping lane to avoid ice. At midnight it struck rocks lying hidden beneath the surface and grounded, gashing the hull. The skipper radioed the Coast Guard for help as large amounts of its oil cargo oil began to leak into the Sound.

Why?
The pilot had, as usual, left the ship after it had left the tricky Valdez Narrows, handing command over to its skipper, Captain Hazelwood. He was unaware of the risk he was running when he decided to deviate from the shipping lane to avoid ice in the channel. With the ship then on automatic pilot he left the third mate in charge of the wheelhouse.

Exxon Valdez was a single-hulled ship and once it had been holed there was nothing to prevent its cargo from escaping.

What happened next?
The grounding had occurred in a very remote place, accessible only by helicopter. By the time help arrived a large amount of oil had already escaped, spreading across the water. Over the coming days, a team was assembled to try and contain and clean up the pollution, but their efforts failed to prevent most of the 10 million gallons of cargo escaping. After three days a storm worsened the conditions.

The oil eventually spread with the tides over an estimated 11,000 square miles, and had damaging effects over 500 miles away. Vast numbers of seabirds and otters perished and the local seafood industry was badly harmed.

The disaster is thought to be the worst ever for its environmental impact, in spite of the fact that some other oil spills – such as the *Torrey Canyon* – were much larger in volume. The clean-up involved use of dispersants, soon found to be ineffective as conditions worsened, then jets of high pressure hot water, together with booms and skimming machines. Exxon is said to have spent some $2 billion on the biggest-ever clean-up operation so far, but even today there are reports of considerable oil contamination remaining along the inaccessible rocky shoreline.

The captain was prosecuted and found guilty of negligent discharge of oil. Exxon is said to have paid out $1 billion in compensation to local communities and appeals against punitive damages awarded by the courts continued for a number of years.

Lessons
The US National Transportation Board identified several factors leading to the grounding of the vessel, finding that the third mate had failed to manoeuvre it properly, possibly because of fatigue; the master of the vessel had failed to provide a proper watch, possibly because he was under the influence of alcohol; the Exxon Shipping Company had failed to supervise the master and provide a rested and sufficient crew; and the US Coast Guard had failed to provide an effective traffic system for vessels in Prince William Sound.

Legislation followed in the US to prevent vessels known to have spilt a million tonnes of oil from entering Prince William Sound and requiring all tankers to be double-hulled by 2015. It is thought that had the *Exxon Valdez* been double-hulled, much of the spill would have been contained.

While it was not wholly effective, the clean-up operation at least showed that some methods were more effective than others and that some could worsen the ecological effects. This experience would at least be relevant to future clean-ups, though it was of little consolation to the residents of Prince William Sound.

Sea Empress, Milford Haven, South Wales, 1996

On 6 January 1993 the tanker *Braer* had lost 65,000 tonnes of crude oil when it hit rocks while drifting in bad weather near the Shetland Islands, the worst pollution incident in the UK since *Torrey Canyon*. The consequences were not as severe as first feared, but three years later a far worse event occurred in British waters.

What happened and why?

During the evening of 19 February 1996, the oil tanker *Sea Empress*, of 147,000 tonnes, ran aground on rocks at Milford Haven, Pembrokeshire, one of the world's largest natural deepwater harbours. As attempts were made to refloat her over the next few days, she spilt 70,000 tonnes of her cargo of North Sea crude oil into the harbour area – considerably more than the 37,000 tonnes lost by the *Exxon Valdez*. A huge slick began to threaten the coastline and its many inlets.

What happened next?

Thousands of seabirds died and even larger numbers of fish, on which the coastal seal population depended for food.

As well as the loss of thousands of tonnes of oil and the heavy cost of the clean-up operation, lasting damage was done to the local economy. In a normal year, half a million people would visit this beautiful part of the Welsh coast. Many were now put off by the pictures beamed into their living rooms of black oil and dead birds washing up on its sandy beaches. It was some years before the coast recovered its recreational reputation.

After investigation by the newly formed Environment Agency, a fine of £1 million was imposed – a record at the time in the British courts for a marine pollution incident.

Lessons

Bad weather obviously makes it more difficult to save a ship crippled by technical breakdown from running aground. In a critical situation 'human factors' can play a positive part and a competent person's intervention may save the situation, although in some of the cases described, mistakes by officers and crew have compounded the difficulties. Improved design and construction of vessels, such as the double hulling of oil tankers to contain cargoes in the event of catastrophe, should help mitigate the consequences.

Sources

Torrey Canyon

Loughborough University. The Torrey Canyon supertanker disaster. www.lboro.ac.uk/
departments/hu/ergsinhu/aboutergs/torrey.html

Smith J E (ed.). *Torrey Canyon pollution and marine life*. Cambridge: Cambridge
University Press, 1968

Amoco Cadiz

Green Nature. Amoco Cadiz oil spill. http://greennature.com/article219.html

Exxon Valdez

National Oceanic and Atmospheric Administration. Emergency response: Exxon Valdez oil
spill. http://response.restoration.noaa.gov/gallery_gallery.php?RECORD KEY%28gallery_
index%29=joinphotogal_id,gallery_id,photo_id&joinphotogal_id%28gallery_index%29=
171&gallery_id%28gallery_index%29=12&photo_id%28gallery_index%29=106

US Environmental Protection Agency. Emergency response: oil spills. www.epa.gov/oilspill/
exxon.htm

Sea Empress

BBC South West Wales. Sea Empress 10 years on. www.bbc.co.uk/wales/southwest/sites/
seaempress

Marine Accident Investigation Branch. *Report of the Chief Inspector of Marine Accidents
into the grounding and subsequent salvage of the tanker SEA EMPRESS*. London: MAIB,
1997. www.archive.official-documents.co.uk/document/dot/seaemp/seaemp.htm

Chapter 12: Offshore catastrophes

Lest we forget
(Title of a play performed in 2009 by the RedRag Theatre Company, Aberdeen, in tribute to the victims of the Piper Alpha disaster)

The North Sea has exacted a heavy toll over the 45 years since we first began drilling its depths for oil and gas. Weather and sea conditions can be extremely hostile, threatening man-made structures; transport to and from the often distant rigs relies on helicopters, with the attendant risks; and extracting oil and gas safely from deep water is technically very challenging, demanding the constant prevention of leaks of volatile hydrocarbons from plant under very high pressure. The men work, eat and sleep in close proximity to these hazards 24 hours a day, and their work is fatiguing. It is not so surprising that many mistakes have been made during the winning of the wealth beneath the waves.

Safety in the North Sea's offshore oil and gas industry left a good deal to be desired in its early years. There was a macho culture and it was clear that offshore safety was relatively lightly regulated compared, say, to coal mining in Great Britain, another very hazardous industry but one which after many years and major disasters had achieved a very mature, strong safety culture.

The responsibility for regulating mining safety, together with the Mines Inspectorate and other safety bodies, had been transferred to the HSE when that new and independent national safety regulator was formed in 1974. On the other hand, the responsibility for enforcing safety offshore was firmly retained by the Department of Energy.

That department was also responsible for sponsoring the industry it was supposed to be policing. Its dual role and the resulting potential conflict of interest were later to be strongly criticised, as was the ineffectualness of its specialised Petroleum Engineering Directorate, which – until Piper Alpha – would remain aloof and isolated from the broader expertise and technical resources of the regulator of onshore safety.

The celebrations of the industry's first oil find in 1965 were soon to be overshadowed by its first disaster.

Sea Gem, North Sea, England, 1965

At around two o'clock in the afternoon on 27 December 1965, 13 men were killed and five injured when British Petroleum's *Sea Gem* drilling rig collapsed and tipped over, throwing them into the icy sea some miles off the Humber estuary.

What happened and why?

The *Sea Gem* was a converted barge, over 200 feet long, which had been fitted with large retractable legs to enable it to steady itself on the sea bottom during drilling operations. The crew were repositioning the rig when, as the legs were being lowered, two suddenly gave way, causing the rig to tilt wildly and then, after about half an hour, turn turtle.

What happened next?

No distress message could be sent as the radio shack had been submerged. But luckily for the survivors, the Chief Engineer of the *Baltrover*, a British cargo ship close by, had seen *Sea Gem* collapsing. A rescue boat was immediately launched and succeeded in saving most of the crew. Helicopters were also summoned to help. Some of the crew had managed to release and board a life raft as the rig tilted, but others hanging on to the part still above water were less fortunate, being catapulted into the sea when the whole installation suddenly turned over. These men perished in the icy water before they could be reached.

By the time the helicopters reached *Sea Gem*, there was only a single leg of the inverted rig to be seen protruding forlornly from the waves.

Lessons

There was much to be learnt from this accident. The offshore industry was very new; the first well producing oil in the North Sea had been drilled only a few weeks earlier, ironically by *Sea Gem* herself. Safety rules were few and would have to be worked out in the light of more accident experience, sadly, in the years to come. But the *Sea Gem* disaster kick-started the process: taking a leaf out of the merchant shipping book, as a result of this disaster every oil and gas installation was required to have an Oil Installation Manager (OIM) in charge, with total authority, like the captain of a ship; and stand-by vessels were always to be present to assist in any emergency requiring evacuation.

Progress towards incorporating safety requirements in legislation for this industry was painfully slow. Eventually, the Mineral Workings (Offshore Installations) Act 1971 required installations to be seaworthy, safe and stable. By then three out of 21 mobile installations had been lost, together with the lives of 20 men.

Alexander Kielland, North Sea, Norway, 1980

Norway's worst offshore accident occurred in 1980, when the drilling rig *Alexander L. Kielland* capsized in the Ekofisk oil field.

What happened?

Built in 1976 in France as a drilling rig, the *Alexander Kielland* had been converted to an accommodation platform (or 'flotel') and hired from its Norwegian owners by the American company Phillips Petroleum. Phillips had moored it alongside their *Edda* oil production platform, where it was used to house the men who worked shifts on *Edda*. The accommodation platform was supported above two semi-submersible floating pontoons by steel legs. For safety reasons it was normal to winch the accommodation away from the production platform every evening until the following day.

This sizeable structure was wrecked within the space of only 14 minutes during the early evening of 27 March 1980, just after the *Alexander Kielland* had been moved away from *Edda*. The weather was bad; it was raining, a gale was blowing with strong gusts of wind, and waves were said by survivors to have been running up to 40 feet high.

The floating platform was anchored by no fewer than six cables. Struck by a massive wave, one of its legs suddenly broke, causing the rig to begin listing badly, putting enormous strain on the anchor cables. Five of these snapped almost at once, leaving just one to hold the rig. As the platform's listing increased this cable also parted, finally causing the platform to capsize.

The *Alexander Kielland* (left) moored alongside the *Edda* oil platform before the accident.
Norsk Oljemuseum

Of the 200 or more men on board, 130 were trapped in the canteen and cinema, upside down and submerged. They had little or no chance of escape.

The platform had been well provided with seven 50-man lifeboats and twenty 20-man rafts, but in these extreme circumstances only four could be launched, and only one of these succeeded in releasing itself from its lowering gear. Ironically, for safety reasons – to prevent premature release during lowering – it was impossible to let go from the lowering gear until all strain on the cables had been relieved.

A fifth lifeboat dropped into the water, went under, and came to the surface upside down. Somehow its occupants managed to right it and save some men in the water. Other men managed to board life rafts that had been thrown into the sea from *Edda*, supply boats plucked others from the sea, and a few saved themselves by swimming to the production platform, an amazing feat in the rough conditions.

However, the standby vessel would take an hour to reach the wrecked installation, by which time there were no more survivors. A total of 123 lives had been lost.

Why did it happen?
The Norwegians appointed a public commission by royal decree to investigate the disaster, and its report was presented to the Ministry of Justice and Police in March 1981. The investigation concluded that the rig collapsed because of a combination of factors, including cold cracks in welds, poor welding and repeated stresses on the structure caused by exposure to extreme North Sea weather. All of this stemmed initially from a manufacturing defect, a welding flaw that led to an undetected fatigue crack in one of the six bracings connecting the leg that collapsed to the rest of the installation.

Remarkably, the origin of that crack was ultimately traced to a poorly welded small fillet joining a non load-bearing flange plate to the bracing, which had been installed to hold a sonar device used during drilling operations. Over time the crack had grown and spread into connected components. The flawed weld appeared to have been painted over during fabrication in the yard.

Moreover, there was no redundancy built into the structure, a design flaw that meant that total collapse was inevitable once the leg had broken in the conditions of that fateful night.

More men might have been saved during the 14 minutes between the first intimation of disaster and the fatal capsize if there had been a better command structure. No one had been clearly in charge and no one had taken control of evacuation.

This was not the first major accident in the Ekofisk field. In 1977 a blow-out on the *Bravo* platform necessitated the evacuation of everyone aboard the installation. Fortunately, on that occasion all survived.

Lessons

The *Alexander Kielland* disaster did at least lead to the tightening of the command system and clarification of roles and responsibilities on offshore installations in the North Sea. Today the Oil Installation Manager (OIM) effectively acts with the same level of authority as the captain of a ship and, properly trained together with the crew, should be competent to cope with foreseeable emergencies.

The design of lifeboats and arrangements for their safe launching have also improved significantly in the wake of lessons learnt from *Piper Alpha* and other North Sea disasters.

But even by the late 1980s, the lessons had not been sufficiently embedded to protect the men working on *Piper Alpha*.

Piper Alpha, North Sea, Scotland, 1988

Until *Piper Alpha*, the worst North Sea accident had been the crash of a Chinook helicopter into the sea between the Brent field and Sumburgh, Shetland, in 1986, when 45 men died and only two survived.

But the safety crunch finally came for both the industry and the Department of Energy on the night of 6 July 1988, when a series of explosions and fires totally destroyed an ageing production platform known as *Piper Alpha*, taking the lives of 167 men, including two crewmen in a rescue boat. There were 59 survivors. Thirty bodies were never recovered.

This appalling event was – and still is – the worst industrial disaster to have occurred in the UK since the Second World War. It is still the worst to have occurred in the offshore industry anywhere in the world. As well as the shocking loss of life, the economic damage was severe. About 10 per cent of UK oil and gas production was lost for a period and the cost of the disaster was estimated at the time as £1.7 billion. How the disaster unfolded, its causes and the steps taken afterwards to reform offshore safety contain lessons that can usefully be applied in other industrial sectors. They are worth relating here in some detail.

What happened?

Piper Alpha was a large fixed platform standing on the seabed in 448 feet of water about 120 miles north of Aberdeen, in the Piper oilfield. Originally built for oil production but later converted to receive gas as well as oil, its operator was Occidental Petroleum (Caledonia) Ltd, a subsidiary of the American company Occidental Petroleum owned by Armand Hammer.

The platform consisted of four modules, with the most hazardous processes separated by fire walls from the accommodation, as was normal good practice. However, this safety principle was ignored when a gas recovery module was added in 1980. The proximity of the gas compression plant to the installation's control room, the heart of *Piper Alpha*'s operational management, was to be a significant factor in escalating the disaster.

The platform received oil and gas from wells in the Piper, Claymore and Tartan fields via pipelines connected to the *Claymore* and *Tartan* platforms. The oil and gas products were transferred from *Piper Alpha* via a 30-inch pipeline to the Flotta terminal in the Orkney Islands, about 130 miles away. This gives some idea of the remoteness of the platform, which was to be significant when it came to the rescue operation.

The facts, as far as they can ever be known, given that the platform was utterly destroyed and so many men died in the inferno, point to an extraordinary sequence of mistakes in which the seeds of the disaster on 7 July 1988 were first sown and then reaped.

The installation had been converted some years earlier to handle both oil and gas, and earlier in 1988 a new gas pipeline had been built. Two condensate pumps, known as Pump A and Pump B, compressed the gas before transmission to Flotta. There were occasionally small leaks from the plant which were not regarded as especially hazardous and the pumps were routinely inspected and maintained every fortnight.

On 6 July, maintenance accordingly began on Pump A during the morning. The pressure safety valve was removed and the condensate pipe was blanked off with a blind flange. That evening, the blank was left in place as the work was not finished; in fact the main overhaul of Pump A had not yet begun. The engineer on duty issued a 'permit' stating that Pump A should not be turned on. Confusingly, another more general permit had been issued relating to the maintenance of Pump A.

The night shift came on at 6 pm. The engineer going off duty did not tell the new shift about Pump A but left the permit forbidding its use in the control room. The plot had taken a fatal twist.

Piper Alpha had a firefighting system consisting of powerful electric and diesel pumps capable of lifting large volumes of sea water. It would normally start automatically in the event of fire. For safety reasons, the system had to be switched to manual when divers were working in the water below so as to protect them from suction at the pumps' inlets. This was the case on the evening of 6 July.

At about 9.45 pm, Pump B stopped and could not be restarted, causing a critical loss of electrical power generation. The manager (or 'custodian') decided it would be necessary to restart Pump A urgently, first checking for permits to work. These were filed in the control room's system for tracking them according to location of plant. Only the general permit for the pump's maintenance work was found; no one knew of the existence of the permit relating to the safety valve as it was in a different plant location file. Assuming it was safe to do so, the manager now restarted Pump A, unaware that this had been forbidden. No one in the vicinity noticed that the safety valve (situated high above the pump) was actually missing.

Pressure immediately began to build up until the blanking flange ruptured. Gas now escaped noisily at high pressure, alerting the men, as sensors began setting off gas alarms. Immediately – and inevitably – the gas cloud found a source of ignition and exploded, the great force destroying the fire wall which had been designed to protect against fire, not explosion. Dashing to the emergency shut off button, the manager closed the valves in the pipelines bringing oil and gas on to the platform, at once stopping all production.

This might still have been the end of the emergency had the local fire which followed the explosion been contained and extinguished. But another fire had started nearby when a flying fragment fractured another condensate pipe. Had adequate blast walls been provided rather than simply firewalls, this might not have happened.

The automatic firefighting system was still turned to manual, and no one started it. The control room, situated too close to the gas recovery plant and no longer protected by the fire wall, had to be evacuated. At this point any chance of managerial command and control evaporated. No tannoy announcements had been made about the fires and the opportunity was gone.

No order to abandon the platform could now be given but following their normal emergency training procedures men tried to reach the lifeboats. But they found that access to these had been cut off by the rapidly developing fires. Awaiting instructions which never came, they took shelter in the accommodation block beneath the helicopter deck which was supposedly protected against fire. Smoke soon began to seep into the accommodation.

Two men went below to try and restart the firefighting system. It did not start and they never returned. Even now *Piper Alpha* might have escaped annihilation had there not been a further, catastrophic turn of events. As they had not been given permission to stop production – always a costly measure – and were at first unaware of the growing crisis, the *Tartan* and *Claymore* platforms were continuing to pump oil to *Piper Alpha*. Pressure built up until more hydrocarbons burst from ruptured pipes, feeding what had by now become a raging inferno. Any vestige of organisation had by now broken down completely. Men began trying to save themselves, some jumping from upper decks into the sea many feet below.

The beginning of the end for *Piper Alpha* came when the high pressure gas line from *Tartan* burst. Tonnes of gas were released and exploded violently in a huge fireball in and around the platform. Yet hope now arrived in the shape of *Tharos*, a firefighting and rescue-dedicated platform. Bravely coming alongside, the crew of *Tharos* attempted to reach the decks, where men could still be seen alive, with its extending walkway. Tragically, this proved to work too slowly. A second massive gas explosion occurred about 20 minutes later as another riser ruptured and *Tharos* was forced to retreat from the intense heat. The platform's end was now in sight as steelwork began melting and the installation began to collapse. Any men left alive on the platform were still sheltering in the doomed accommodation or were jumping into the icy waves far below.

At about 10.30 pm *Claymore* stopped pumping oil but by then it was too late to make a difference. The pipeline between *Piper Alpha* and *Claymore* now burst, the fire raged on, and the module containing the accommodation block collapsed into the sea. As dawn broke on 7 July little was left of the wreckage, still burning under a vast pall of smoke.

Of the 226 people on the platform that night, only 61 made it to safety. Helicopters had been unable to land on the platform's helideck during the fire because of the wind-driven smoke and intense heat. A total of 167 men died, including the two crew members of a rescue boat that had been engulfed by the first fireball, together with the six men they had saved from the sea.

Why?
The bare facts set out above speak volumes about what went wrong and why: there were inherent design flaws, system and procedural failures surrounding maintenance and permit to work procedures, communication problems between shifts and a lack of leadership once the control room had been destroyed, resulting in failures to bring the local fire under control, communicate properly with the whole workforce and command an orderly evacuation when that proved impossible. That *Claymore* and *Tartan* continued pumping for so long in spite of being able to see the fire tragically made matters far worse, and may well have stemmed from the kind of culture that puts production before safety.

What happened next?
A public inquiry was set up in November 1988 to establish the cause of the disaster. Two years later the Cullen Report was published; its recommendations would shape the future of safety management in the offshore and other major hazard industries. It would also make a dramatic difference to the way they were regulated.

The memorial to the victims of *Piper Alpha* in Hazlehead Park, Aberdeen.
Chris Nixon

Lord Cullen concluded that the immediate cause of the catastrophe was a gas leak resulting from maintenance work being carried out simultaneously on the condensate pump and its related safety valve. He made 106 recommendations for changes to North Sea safety procedures, all of which were accepted by the industry. One of these was to the government: drawing attention to the conflict of interest in having production and safety overseen by the same agency, he recommended that the responsibility for enforcing safety in the North Sea should be transferred from the Department of Energy to the HSE, the independent national safety regulator.

The inquiry criticised *Piper Alpha*'s operator, Occidental Petroleum, for having inadequate maintenance and safety procedures. But no criminal charges were brought against the company. Occidental left the North Sea after the disaster, never to return.

Near misses, successes and failures since *Piper Alpha*
There have been some dramatic near misses in the North Sea. I recall visiting the floating production, storage and offloading (FPSO) ship *Schiehallion*, anchored in the exposed waters off Shetland, with inspectors from the HSE's offshore safety division not long after a massive wave – the '50-year wave' – had struck the vessel's bow, almost rupturing it. The damage was impressive but the steel hull's integrity had held, averting disaster. Use of such vessels was controversial, as it was novel technology,

and they would often be exposed to threatening weather conditions. Ten years later, the vessel is due for replacement.

And there have been successes too, thanks to investment in the training of a competent workforce. I recall my helicopter survival training course in Aberdeen. Being dunked into the heavily chlorinated water of the practice tank, clad in a bulky survival suit was unpleasant enough. As the machine rolled and sank, filling with water, remembering the drill was not as easy as it sounds. With divers on hand to help, there was no danger of being trapped. It was reassuring to have been taught what to do, but I wondered what it would be like in the icy North Sea in February, in a Force 9 gale.

On several occasions men have survived ditching. In February 2009 at 6.40 pm the alarm was raised when a Super Puma helicopter came down in the North Sea near a BP oil platform in the ETAP field, 125 miles east of Aberdeen. Flotation chambers inflated on impact and the helicopter remained upright. All 18 passengers and crew members survived the impact, the sea conditions were mild and the men were able to step out of the floating helicopter into life rafts that had automatically deployed and inflated after the ditching.

Flares were seen from the BP platform, and life jacket lights were spotted by the search and rescue teams. The rescue was assisted by the rafts being equipped with locator beacons, enabling their position to be pinpointed in the dark. Rougher conditions that night might well have caused the helicopter to capsize, but if so the men's training would have given them a good chance of survival.

Not so fortunate, however, were the seven men who died when a helicopter carrying workers to the gas platforms crashed into Morecambe Bay in 2007, nor the 16 lost from a helicopter that came down in good weather in the North Sea on 1 April 2009.

Lessons

Twenty years on from *Piper Alpha*, oil and gas continues to be produced from the North Sea, aided by better technology: the industry has developed techniques such as slant drilling that have enabled dwindling reserves to be maximised long after the fields were expected to be exhausted. Although offshore safety has undoubtedly improved since Lord Cullen's recommendations were adopted, accidents have continued to occur. In 2007 three crewmen were killed on board a rig support vessel. There have been near-miss collisions between moving vessels and installations which could have had serious consequences. And a constantly wary eye has to be kept out for hydrocarbon leaks.

So-called 'gleaners' – smaller companies – are now taking over some of the fields where the low-hanging fruits were first taken by the oil majors. It remains to be seen whether the safety standards achieved in recent years can be maintained. While the injury statistics have improved, the ever-present risks of fire, explosion and structural collapse remain.

The HSE has warned that an increasing number of the floating rigs are now beyond their planned life by as much as 10 years, and need increasing maintenance. There are also concerns that the industry is facing difficult times, with the cost of extracting the gas and oil left beneath British waters increasing as reserves begin to run down.

While the industry asserts that it aims to become the safest offshore sector in the world, trade unions remain sceptical, believing it is not learning lessons and is only paying lip-service to the safety and wellbeing of the workforce. However, it is encouraging that the latest figures published by the HSE for 2008/09 show that – not including the loss of 17 workers in related air transport and maritime accidents – no workers were killed on installations for the second consecutive year and the combined fatal and major injury incidence rate continued its recent downward trend.

There will never be room for complacency.

Sources

Sea Gem
Britain: Sinking of the *Sea Gem*. *Time*, 7 January 1966. www.time.com/time/magazine/article/0,9171,834965,00.html
Dukes Wood Oil Museum. Sea Gem. www.dukeswoodoilmuseum.co.uk/sea_gem.htm

Alexander Kielland
Norwegian Government. *The Alexander L Kielland accident. Report of a Norwegian public commission appointed by royal decree of March 28, 1980, presented to the Ministry of Justice and Police*. Oslo, 1981
Norwegian Petroleum Museum. The black days. http://stavanger.clickwalk.no/cgi-bin/seq.cgi?id=133&by=stavanger&lang=1&ttype=3

Piper Alpha
Cullen, The Hon. Lord. *The Public Inquiry into the Piper Alpha disaster*. London: HMSO, 1990

General
Step Change in Safety (UK oil and gas safety partnership). http://stepchangeinsafety.net/stepchange

Chapter 13: Aviation accidents

Once you have flown, you will walk the earth with your eyes turned
skyward, for there you have been, there you long to return.
(Leonardo da Vinci, 1452–1519)

Not everyone shares Leonardo's passion for aviation. While his drawings
foresaw a future in which mankind would fly, there is nothing that
suggests that he also predicted flying disasters. Some people have a terrible
fear of flying accidents and will never board an aircraft in spite of the tens
of thousands of flights that take place safely every year. And human and
technical failures do occur from time to time in the aviation industry,
sometimes with horrific results.

The aircraft collision at Tenerife, Canary Islands, 1977

One of the world's worst aviation disasters occurred in the early evening
of Sunday 27 March 1977 on an airport runway in the Canary Islands,
when two Boeing 747-400 Jumbo Jet aircraft collided.

What happened?

A Pan Am Clipper that had just arrived at Los Rodeos airport in Tenerife
was taxiing in fog on the runway when it was struck by a KLM Jumbo
attempting to take off. Both planes had been diverted to Los Rodeos from
Las Palmas, where a terrorist bomb had exploded.

The aftermath of the
collision at Tenerife
airport, 27 March
1977.
Topfoto

Why?

Los Rodeos was a small airport with only a single runway for take-off and landing and a parallel taxiway which was full of parked planes that had already been diverted. The weather conditions that evening were foggy and visibility was poor. A terrible mix-up followed. Because the taxiway was crowded, after landing safely the Pan Am Clipper was given permission by the control tower to taxi back down the single runway, turn off at a particular exit, and park. The message reached the Clipper as it passed an exit, and the crew assumed it referred to another. The crew continued taxiing down the runway.

The KLM plane which had also been in touch with the control tower was already on the runway, in position ready to take off. Neither aircraft could be seen by the control tower. Misunderstood messages now passed between air traffic control and the KLM flight which the crew interpreted as authorising them to go. Unable in the murky conditions to see the Pan Am plane taxiing towards them, still looking for the exit, the KLM began accelerating down the runway.

What happened next?

Too late, the KLM pilots saw the approaching aircraft. As the Pan Am Clipper now desperately tried to get out of the way the KLM 747 attempted to become airborne – and almost made it. It ploughed along the Clipper's roof before crashing to the ground and coming to rest some distance away, upside down and on fire. The stricken Pan Am aircraft also erupted in flames. Each plane soon became an inferno. There was no escape for 583 people who died in the blazing wreckage, belted into their seats.

Miraculously, 61 people in the Pan Am plane managed to survive the appalling collision. One man climbed out through a hole ripped in the roof by the KLM plane's undercarriage. His only injury was a broken ankle when he slid off the wing to the ground. There were no KLM survivors.

Lessons

There had been a fateful combination of factors that day: the unusual volume of traffic at a small airport without ground radar, poor visibility due to fog, possible anxiety by the KLM captain to get away before the weather closed in, use of unclear language and a misunderstanding between him and the control tower, the Pan Am pilots' desperate radio calls lost during the confused exchange going on between the tower and the KLM plane, and a single channel radio telephone system unable to cope with multiple simultaneous transmissions.

Changes were made to international regulations governing commercial aviation as a result of this terrible disaster, including a requirement that in future only clear, standard phrases in English should be used in communications between air traffic control and aircraft. Ground radar was installed at Los Rodeos.

The Kegworth air crash, Leicestershire, England, 1989

Human factors also led to an avoidable disaster near East Midlands Airport in the UK when British Midland Flight BM 92, on its way from London Heathrow to Belfast with 118 passengers and a crew of eight on board, crashed into the embankment of the M1 motorway. It was a classic case of mechanical breakdown combined with a communications failure and human error.

What happened?

On 8 January 1989 a fan blade failed in the port side jet engine of the twin engined plane while it was still climbing towards its cruising height. There was a good deal of vibration felt, some passengers could see smoke and flames coming from the port side engine, and smoke began to enter the main cabin though the air conditioning system.

Why?

However, this information was not relayed by the cabin crew to the captain and his first officer. Used to an earlier version of the aircraft, they

The air crash on the M1 embankment near Kegworth, January 1989.
Popperfoto/ Getty Images

could also feel the vibration and smell the smoke but from their experience of the earlier variant believed it must be the starboard engine that was in trouble. They decided to shut it down.

The cabin crew had assumed the pilots could see smoke and flames from the port side engine. In fact they were unable to see either engine from the cockpit but after they had shut down the starboard engine were reassured by the fact that they could no longer smell smoke. They believed they had shut down the defective engine and that the remaining engine would enable them to land at a nearby airport.

What happened next?
The pilots alerted British Midland to their problem and the flight was diverted to East Midlands Airport, adjacent to the M1 motorway.

However, fuel was still being pumped into the defective port side engine, which now erupted into flames and failed completely. With neither engine running, the plane was rapidly losing height. Realising that the wrong engine had been shut down, the pilots tried to restart it. Attempts failed. Now with no power but trying to avoid a crash landing in the village of Kegworth the captain prepared to land by gliding onto the runway at East Midlands Airport. This heroic attempt failed by a matter of only a few feet. Within sight of the runway but just without sufficient height to make it, the aircraft ploughed into the high embankment of the M1 motorway.

Miraculously, no traffic on the motorway was involved and all members of the flight crew survived the impact, though sadly 47 passengers died. There were 79 survivors, many seriously injured.

Lessons
The vibration experienced had been a symptom of engine malfunction associated with metal fatigue in the fan blades, which the manufacturers were soon able to put right. The official report of the inquiry into the disaster made 31 recommendations, leading to many improvements in aircraft safety.

Human factors were critical. A mechanical failure can often be successfully overcome by human intervention. Unfortunately, failures in human communication and understanding can sometimes compound the problem. On this occasion it was disastrous.

The Concorde crash, Paris, 2000
The future of the first commercial jet airliner, the much admired De Havilland Comet, looked bleak when metal fatigue in the wings was

found to have caused a crash in 1954. But the plane returned to service after this problem was solved and flew commercially for many years. It is still flying today in the much modified form of the RAF's Nimrod reconnaissance aircraft, 70 years since the Comet's first flight.

However, another iconic aircraft, the first airliner to travel faster than the speed of sound, faced the end of its long commercial life, in spite of having one of the finest safety records, soon after a disastrous crash in Paris.

What happened and why?
On 25 July 2000, at around five o'clock in the evening, an Air France Concorde flight took off from Paris Charles de Gaulle airport for New York. But as it cleared the airport perimeter, it was seen to be trailing a dcnsc black plume of smoke and flames.

With one of its engines on fire, Concorde was struggling to maintain speed. The undercarriage was still down, damaged and slowing the aircraft, and the crew tried in vain to retract it. As its engines faltered, the doomed aircraft began to lose height. Within minutes of take-off, it crashed into the nearby Hôtelissimo hotel, killing all 109 passengers and crew and four people on the ground.

Arguments have continued ever since about possible causes of the crash, including the possibility that rubber fragments flung from a tyre bursting during take-off could have ruptured a fuel tank in the wing. The controversy may be settled at a hearing in a French court during 2010, by which time 10 years will have elapsed since the event.

What happened next?
Although grounded for a period while modifications were made, Concorde was then allowed to continue to fly, but after the terrorist attacks of 11 September 2001, its transatlantic business waned. Commercial pressures finally led to decisions by British Airways and Air France to cease Concorde services, sadly marking the end of an era of civilian supersonic travelling.

Lessons
A striking feature of the aviation industry is its 'no blame' culture which encourages aircrew to report near misses and other events that could have a bearing on safety. For example, the British Air Accidents Investigation Branch runs a 'Confidential Human Factors Incident Reporting Programme' (CHIRP) that enables mistakes to be reported and analysed without recriminations. This is a model that could usefully be adopted by other industrial sectors.

Sources

Tenerife

1977: Hundreds dead in Tenerife air crash. BBC News Online: On this day, 27 March. http://news.bbc.co.uk/onthisday/hi/dates/stories/march/27/newsid_2531000/2531063.stm

Aviation Safety Network. Accident description, 27 March 1977: Pan American World Airways N736PA. http://aviation-safety.net/database/record.php?id=19770327-0

Smith P. Ask the pilot. A look back at the catastrophic chain of events that caused history's deadliest plane crash 30 years ago. *Salon*, 6 April 2007. www.salon.com/tech/col/smith/2007/04/06/askthepilot227

Kegworth

Air Accidents Investigation Branch. *Report on the accident to Boeing 737-400, G-OBME, near Kegworth, Leicestershire on 8 January 1989* (Report 4/1990). www.aaib.gov.uk/publications/formal_reports/4_1990_g_obme.cfm

BBC News Online. Kegworth: 10 years on. http://news.bbc.co.uk/1/hi/uk/250959.stm

Paris

Bureau d'enquêtes et d'analyses pour la sécurité de l'aviation civile. *Accident on 25 July 2000 at La Patte d'Oie in Gonesse (95) to the Concorde registered F-BTSC operated by Air France.* Paris: BEA, 2002. www.bea-fr.org/docspa/2000/f-sc000725a/pdf/f-sc000725a.pdf

Chapter 14: Catastrophes in space

We will never forget them, nor the last time we saw them, this morning, as they prepared for their journey and waved goodbye and 'slipped the surly bonds of Earth' to 'touch the face of God'.
(From the poem quoted by President Reagan in his address to the nation after the *Challenger* disaster)

The dramas and tragedies associated with the exploration of space over the last 50 years convey many lessons that remain universally applicable to understanding the role and responsibilities of anyone managing risks today. The story begins with the US spacecraft known as *Apollo 1*.

The *Apollo 1* disaster, USA, 1967
NASA's lunar exploration Apollo programme had an inauspicious start with a disastrous blaze that destroyed the spacecraft *Apollo 1* on its launch pad during a test and training exercise on 27 January 1967. Three astronauts perished in the fire.

An internal inquiry conducted by a board led by NASA's research director identified design flaws as possible causes, including an oxygen rich (100 per cent) atmosphere, the presence of flammable materials in the cockpit, an inward-opening escape hatch and the insufficient protection offered by the astronauts' suits.

Fire damage to the *Apollo 1* module, January 1967.
NASA

Damage to *Apollo 13*,
April 1970.
NASA

Some safety lessons had clearly been taken on board successfully by the time the first manned mission to the Moon, *Apollo 11*, landed triumphantly and returned safely in July 1969.

'A successful failure' – *Apollo 13*, USA, 1970
Apollo 13's mission was not so successful, though its safe return was hailed as a huge triumph over what had seemed inevitably fatal circumstances.

Launched on 11 April 1970, *Apollo 13* was NASA's third manned lunar landing mission. Two days into the flight, an electrical fault in a stirrer motor caused an explosion in an oxygen tank in a service module, causing loss of oxygen and electrical power. "Houston, we've had a problem" made the news throughout the world that night.

The crew's situation was dire and their future looked bleak. The command module had only a limited supply of oxygen and electricity. However, they were advised that if they shut down the command module they could enter the lunar landing module which had its own independent supplies. Although it had not been designed for the purpose, in theory it seemed possible they could use it to return to Earth and land.

Despite great hardship caused by severely limited power, heat in the restricted space of the cabin, and lack of drinking water, the crew managed a safe return to Earth in the lunar landing module. The mission eventually became known as a 'successful failure'.

Sadly it would be impossible to use those words about the disaster that occurred to the Space Shuttle *Challenger* 16 years later.

The *Challenger* disaster, USA, 1986

On 28 January 1986 I found myself snowbound in Surrey with friends watching the launch of the US Space Shuttle *Challenger* on television. It was about half past eleven in the morning at the Kennedy Space Center in Florida, where it was a sunny but unusually cold day following heavy frost on previous nights.

As usual, and in spite of the cold, an eager crowd had assembled there to witness the launch. NASA had billed this space mission as truly momentous as a civilian woman had been chosen to be a crew member, the first from the Teachers in Space Project. Tragically, it would turn out to be momentous for all the wrong reasons.

What happened?

The sight of the rocket lifting off in the sunshine into the clear blue sky, belching a plume of smoke and flame, was truly spectacular. The television commentator was chattering excitedly and everything seemed fine as it soared away.

The Space Shuttle *Challenger* explodes shortly after launch, 28 January 1986. *NASA*

Seventy-three seconds later, the shuttle exploded. Fragments began spiralling down towards the sea, trailing a zigzag pattern of white smoke. Everyone watching was stunned and appalled by the fate of *Challenger*'s seven crew members. Television ensured that the awful scene was witnessed by millions of watching eyes across the world.

Why?
The immediate technical cause was the failure of a single safety-critical component. The space shuttle consisted of several elements: an orbiter vehicle (named *Challenger*) containing the crew, a large externally mounted rocket fuel tank containing liquid hydrogen fuel and liquid oxygen oxidiser, and two solid rocket boosters. The solid rocket booster engines were formed from six separate sections, whose joints were sealed by rubber O-rings to prevent gas leakage from the solid fuel motor. One of these failed, allowing a jet of extremely hot, pressurised gas to escape and play heat like a cutting torch onto the external fuel tank. Within seconds this tank had been penetrated and its fuel contents ignited. The liquid hydrogen and oxygen exploded with massive force, instantly wrecking the shuttle.

So much for the technical failure. The root causes were at first less clear but investigation proved them to be all too familiar.

What happened next?
After the fire on the *Apollo 1* launch pad in 1967, NASA had been allowed to conduct its own internal investigation. This time it was clear that an independent inquiry was needed.

The space shuttle programme was suspended for the next 32 months as President Reagan announced a special commission of inquiry to investigate why the disaster had occurred, led by William P Rogers, the former US Secretary of State. After sitting for months and interviewing many witnesses, the 'Rogers Commission' found that NASA's organisational culture and decision-making processes had been key factors contributing to the catastrophe.

For various reasons, the launch had already had to be put back several times. The cold weather had caused the latest setback. It seems that the fate of *Challenger* and its crew was sealed the evening before the launch, when NASA staff ignored concerns raised by engineers at Morton Thiokol, the rocket motor contractor, about the risk of O-ring failure in such cold conditions and failed to report those concerns to senior managers. Contrary to any perception that NASA always put safety first, they felt they were under strong pressure to agree to go ahead.

The main contractor, Rockwell, had also become alarmed by the build-up of ice that had occurred on the fixed structure adjoining the space vehicle in spite of the efforts of a team employed overnight to remove it. The risk was of ice breaking loose during launch and striking the shuttle, damaging its heat protection tiles. However, after discussion the NASA official responsible for deciding a launch allowed an hour's delay for further inspection. When he was told that the ice appeared to be melting, he decided to go ahead.

Lessons

A disaster such as this incurs enormous cost in terms of damaged reputation as well as precious lives. NASA's space programme was set back several years by the *Challenger* disaster. There were to be no more manned lunar landings.

The *Challenger* disaster is a sad tale not simply of flaws in design and the failure of safety critical components, but of a deceptively inadequate safety culture in a high risk operation, allowing people to make wrong decisions by succumbing to pressure. It has become a classic case study of the ethics that govern decisions about safety, with which everyone who has responsibilities for safety needs to be familiar.

The client NASA and a contractor both failed to deal adequately with a known design flaw likely to lead to the failure of a safety-critical component in low temperature launching conditions. It is vital to ensure optimal operating conditions when risks to life are so high. Pressure to act in the face of expert advice to the contrary has to be strongly resisted by engineers and managers; only a robust corporate safety culture will give decision-makers the confidence to do this.

The Rogers Commission made nine recommendations that were to be implemented by NASA before shuttle flights resumed. One of these was that the agency must undertake a total redesign of the solid rocket boosters, overseen by an independent board.

Seventeen years passed before another catastrophe raised fresh doubts about the strength of NASA's safety culture.

The *Columbia* disaster, USA, 2003

The *Columbia*'s crew of seven was killed on 1 February 2003 when the orbiter broke up on re-entry before landing. Protective heat-resistant tiles covering a wing had been damaged during the launch, when they had been struck by a piece of foam insulation that broke away from an external fuel tank. This incident had been observed but NASA had decided it did not jeopardise the flight.

Examining the underlying causes of this second space shuttle disaster, the Columbia Accident Investigation Board (CAIB), in an enquiry led by Admiral Harold Gehman, concluded that NASA had failed to learn many of the lessons of the *Challenger* disaster, pointing out that it had not set up a fully independent unit for the supervision of safety, as intended by the Rogers Commission. The CAIB also believed that "the causes of the institutional failure responsible for *Challenger* have not been fixed", saying that the same "flawed decision-making process" identified by Rogers in 1986 was responsible for the destruction of the *Columbia* in 2003.

Sources

Apollo 1
Benson C D and Faherty W B. (1978). *Moonport: a history of Apollo launch facilities and operations*. NASA History Series: NASA Special Publication 4204. Washington, DC: NASA, 1978. www.hq.nasa.gov/office/pao/History/SP-4204/contents.html
National Aeronautics and Space Administration. Apollo 1 (204). www.hq.nasa.gov/office/pao/History/Apollo204

Apollo 13
MSC Apollo 13 Investigation Team. *Spacecraft incident investigation*. Washington, DC: NASA, 1970
National Aeronautics and Space Administration. Apollo 13 mission details. http://science.ksc.nasa.gov/history/apollo/apollo-13/apollo-13.html

Challenger
National Aeronautics and Space Administration. Challenger STS 51-L accident. http://history.nasa.gov/sts51l.html
Rogers W P. *Report of the Presidential Commission on the Space Shuttle Challenger accident*. Washington, DC: NASA, 1986. http://history.nasa.gov/rogersrep/genindex.htm

Columbia
Columbia Accident Investigation Board. http://caib.nasa.gov

Chapter 15: Nuclear disasters

The very word 'nuclear' holds a dread for society, being associated so negatively with the development of the atomic bombs used in the raids on Hiroshima and Nagasaki. Associated with 'disaster' it becomes a 'double whammy'.

The civil nuclear story is far more positive, though marred by some calamities that owe more to human stupidity than malice. Numerous relatively minor events have occurred in the civil nuclear industry, but these pale into insignificance compared with the fire at Great Britain's Windscale plant in 1957, the near meltdown at Three Mile Island in Pennsylvania in 1979 and the explosion at Chernobyl in 1986.

The Windscale fire, England, 1957

Had the fire at the experimental nuclear piles at Windscale occurred today, all hell would have broken loose. In those days, things were kept a little quieter. Even so – make no mistake – this was a major disaster.

Windscale (later rebranded as Sellafield) lies in a remote area of beautiful Cumbria, beside the Irish Sea. Originally a military installation established to help the UK achieve its status as a military nuclear power, by the mid-1950s Windscale was emerging from the postwar twilight as the home of Britain's civil nuclear generating industry. Britain's first civil nuclear power station, Calder Hall, was opened by the Queen in 1956. Today, as well as the legacies of wartime experimentation, the extensive site houses a nuclear fuel reprocessing plant and some of the most up-to-date nuclear facilities in the world.

What happened and why?

On 10 April 1957 one of the two experimental nuclear 'piles', as they were then known (the nuclear reactors), began overheating. The reactors' purpose was to produce plutonium for military purposes.

Windscale Piles 1 and 2 were contained in two towering concrete chimney-like structures, 400 feet high, with large filtration galleries mounted on top. For years these have been brooding icons of Britain's nuclear landscape. At the base of these structures sat the reactors with solid, air-cooled graphite cores.

The hot air created by the cooling process was vented up the chimney to the atmosphere via the filters. The filters were almost an afterthought, deemed unnecessary and expensive by some engineers at the time, but not

Workers involved in
the clean-up after the
Windscale accident,
1957.
Topfoto

by Sir John Cockcroft, their designer. He may well have prevented a disaster from becoming a catastrophe.

When the piles had been designed little was known about the effects of Wigner energy, named after its Hungarian discoverer. Energy is released in the form of heat when graphite is exposed to neutrons. When the piles began operating, it was thought that this might account for the higher than desired temperatures experienced during operation of the piles. An annealing process was believed to be the solution, whereby the cores would be deliberately heated to higher than normal temperature, allowing the Wigner energy to dissipate gently. At least, that was the theory. It was discovered that as time went on, higher and higher temperatures were required to achieve the desired result. An accident was waiting to happen.

It is still not certain today what caused the accident. Several design flaws in these early reactors probably contributed. Some say a fuel can caught fire – the fuel was metallic uranium, not today's uranium oxide, and it burns if overheated. There was also a fire hazard present from the combination of graphite and cooling air (graphite burns in air) and any radioactive particles not trapped by the filters would vent to the atmosphere. The annealing process was not monitored effectively as the thermocouples installed for annealing purposes could not measure the temperature throughout the reactor core.

In the event, it was the fuel which caught fire, not the graphite, but none of this had been foreseen.

Early on 10 October, in spite of a second annealing process which had begun on 8 October following the failure of a previous attempt, instruments were showing that the reactor in Pile 1 was still heating, not cooling as intended. The operators' response was to increase the flow of cooling air. This made matters worse. Suddenly it became apparent that radiation monitors in the filters were reading off the scale. A site emergency was immediately declared.

By now the fuel was glowing red hot. Operators standing on top of the reactor building could see fuel cartridges glowing at the back of the reactor where cooling air discharged to the flues. Soon this had become an inferno, with extreme heat endangering the structure.

As cooling had failed, no one knew how to deal with this situation. According to witnesses, the burning fuel was now white hot. Carbon dioxide was injected in an attempt to extinguish the fire, but proved useless. Precious hours were passing.

By Friday 11 October, 11 tonnes of uranium fuel were on fire. The reactor temperature was now so high that the entire structure was at risk of collapse. Desperate measures were necessary.

No one knew whether pouring water onto the blaze from above would work. There was certainly a huge risk of explosion. But there was nothing else for it but to try. Operators showed enormous courage in risking their lives to prevent further catastrophe and, incredibly, as hundreds of gallons were pumped in, their superhuman efforts were rewarded as the flames subsided. Water was kept flowing for another 24 hours until the reactor was completely cool.

No one was believed to have been immediately harmed by this event, but according to estimates at least 20,000 curies of radioactive material was released, including iodine-131, which can cause thyroid cancer. It was feared that milk might be contaminated.

What happened next?

An inquiry into the incident was promptly launched, led by the highly respected Sir William Penney. Remarkably, compared with the snail's pace of modern inquiries, Penney reported on 26 October. He declared that the primary cause of the accident had been the second annealing on 8 October, applied too soon and too rapidly. He was complimentary about the action taken to bring the fire under control, considered that the measures taken to deal with its consequences were adequate, and that there had been no immediate damage to the health of workers or the general public. However, he criticised technical and organisational deficiencies and called for an assessment which would lead to changes in organisation, clearer definition of responsibilities and better definition of radiation dose limits.

Lessons

Things would have turned out far worse had the fire not been brought under control. In terms of the off-site radiation doses, the consequences still remain unclear. The Irish and Isle of Man governments feared that wind had blown the escaping radioactive particles across the Irish Sea. However, in England the general public seemed not to be over-concerned; there was a fuss in the popular press but it did not seem to the public that a major disaster had occurred, though of course it had. Politically, unlike the effect that Three Mile Island was to have later in the USA, the Windscale fire was not an impediment to the subsequent building of nuclear power stations around Britain's coasts. But at least one lesson had been learnt. No more air-cooled reactors were built.

Windscale Pile 1 had been wrecked beyond repair in the blaze; how to safely dismantle and dispose of its remains, which included thousands of fuel rods and isotope containers, was to puzzle engineers for decades to follow. Half a century later work is finally in progress to remove the contaminated core and demolish the structure. Windscale Pile 2 was shut down and never restarted. The risk was just too great.

Three Mile Island, Pennsylvania, 1979

The Windscale fire was the worst reactor disaster in the world until the incident at Three Mile Island in 1979.

What happened?

In March 1979, exactly one year after its first start-up, a partial meltdown occurred in Reactor Number 2, one of the two pressurised water nuclear reactors (PWRs) at Three Mile Island (TMI) Nuclear Generating Station situated near Harrisburg, Pennsyslvania. This was the worst accident to have occurred in the American civil nuclear power industry, releasing over a populated area an estimated 43,000 curies of radioactive krypton, though less than 20 curies of iodine-131 (compare the estimated release during the Windscale fire).

Why?

PWRs depend on the constant circulation of water both to create steam to drive the power generating turbines and for cooling purposes, in three separate loops controlled via a system of pumps and valves. The reactor is situated in a 'containment' structure. Water is pumped through the reactor core in a pressurised primary loop, and superheated. Via a heat exchanger, this heat enables a separate supply of feed water to be converted into dry steam by a steam generator. The dry steam is carried away by a secondary loop which transfers it to the steam turbine. As the steam drives the turbine and loses its energy it is then transferred via a third, condensing, loop from the turbine to a separate cooling tower before being recycled to the steam generator as feed water. It is vital to the safe operation of the plant that all these stages function normally; if there is a failure anywhere the plant is designed to shut down safely.

On 29 March 1979, during normal operation at four o'clock in the morning, a pump failure caused feed water to stop flowing through the secondary loop, which meant that heat was no longer being removed from the reactor via the primary loop and heat exchanger. In the absence of steam the turbine shut down, followed by the reactor, as designed. Pressure began to increase in the primary loop, but this was to be expected during shut-down. So far, so good.

This pressure was controlled normally by a pressuriser situated above the reactor. To prevent pressure from becoming excessive, a relief valve was designed to open automatically. It did so. However, it was now that things began to go wrong. The valve should have closed again after the pressure had been released to restore the level to normal, but it remained open. The operators mistakenly believed that it had closed because their instrumentation told them that a signal to close the valve had been sent to it. There was no signal to tell them that it was still open. One thing was now to lead to another.

Because the operators mistakenly assumed the valve was closed, it was allowed to remain open for several hours. Pressure continued to fall, accompanied by loss of cooling water which was escaping through the valve into a sump, unnoticed. The reactor core slowly began to overheat.

What happened next?

A series of mistakes by operators followed, allowing the incident to escalate. According to the US Nuclear Regulatory Commission's (NRC) subsequent investigation, the operators missed several opportunities to arrest the situation because they were misled by their instrumentation.

The operators at first failed to recognise that they were dealing with a loss of coolant. Surprisingly, there was no instrument in the control room showing the level of cooling water in the reactor. They mistakenly assumed that if there was water in the pressuriser – and its instrumentation led them to believe that there was – there would be water in the reactor. However, they did not know that the level gauge was giving a false reading because of the effect of the open valve.

There was a back-up system to provide feed water in an emergency, but it failed, ironically because it had been tested a day or two before the accident. Valves on the emergency feed water lines to the steam generator had been deliberately closed for the purpose of the test. They should have been reopened at its conclusion, but this safety-critical step had somehow been overlooked.

However, the operators spotted this failure within minutes and were able to restore the supply of feed water to the steam generator. To their consternation it did not have the cooling effect desired. By now, because voids had formed in the secondary loop, the feed water was not flowing properly. This was preventing the reactor's heat from escaping through the primary loop and heat exchanger. The voids now caused the pressuriser's level gauge to indicate (erroneously) that the water level was rising, which misled the operators into turning off the supply. The puzzled operators remained unaware that the amount of water in the system was steadily decreasing and that the reactor was overheating as its core became uncovered.

Meanwhile, radioactive coolant still discharging from the open valve had filled the sump and was overflowing into the containment building, setting off an alarm. Together with other indications such as excessive temperature on the discharge line from the valve, this should have indicated a loss of coolant, but these signs were still missed by the operators.

After about two hours the top of the reactor core was exposed, generating intense heat. The fuel rods began to be damaged, releasing more radioactivity into the remaining coolant and producing hydrogen, later to cause a small explosion in the containment building.

After a shift change in the control room at 6 am the penny finally dropped and it was realised that the plant was experiencing a major accident. By then about 250,000 gallons of radioactive coolant had been lost from the primary loop, heavily contaminating the plant. The coolant's radiation level was now about 300 times above normal. A 'Site Area Emergency' (the NRC's second highest accident level) was declared and shortly afterwards upgraded to a 'General Emergency' (the highest accident level).

The control room staff still did not know that the primary loop's water level was low, nor that more than half the core was now exposed, but after taking samples from the primary loop which showed that the radiation levels were three times above normal, the pumps were turned on again and the reactor temperature at last began to fall. The incident was at last under control but a week was to pass before it was over. A senior executive of the operating company was reported to have described it as a "normal aberration". There was no emergency evacuation of the local population (25,000 people lived within a few miles of the site). It was not until later, when it was discovered that half of the reactor had been severely damaged, that the enormity of what might have occurred began to dawn.

President Carter swiftly ordered an inquiry into the incident. The Kemeny Commission Report concluded that: "There will either be no case of cancer or the number of cases will be so small that it will never be possible to detect them. The same conclusion applies to the other possible health effects."

The State of Pennsylvania's preparedness for a nuclear accident was criticised by local politicians because the authorities did not keep potassium iodide in stock (to protect the thyroid gland in the event of exposure to radioactive iodine).

Lessons
The environmental clean-up operation that followed took several years and cost nearly $1 trillion. It would be many more years before any nuclear power plants that had not already been ordered were constructed in the USA: the incident at TMI was probably a major factor, though others, such as the availability of cheap gas, were coming into play. What is clear is that the disaster did nothing to improve international public confidence in the safety of nuclear power.

Intelligent human beings can easily be misled into wrong actions by instrumentation. The mistaken reliance on a misleading indication from the level gauge on the pressuriser was a significant contributing factor, but water level gauges on the reactor vessel might have prevented the accident.

Both the Windscale and TMI incidents were eclipsed by the catastrophe at Chernobyl in the Soviet Union.

The Chernobyl explosion, Ukraine, 1986

On the weekend of the Chernobyl disaster my wife and I were visiting Kraków with friends and we spent some hours several hundred feet below ground in a salt mine, blissfully unaware that a vast plume of radioactivity was drifting across the Polish border from Ukraine. Though we did not know it then, the mine was probably the safest place to be for miles around. It was not until we were flying home that we were told anything about the worst nuclear accident ever to have occurred.

What happened?

During an experiment which went badly wrong in the early hours of 26 April 1986, Reactor Number 4 at the Chernobyl nuclear power plant exploded catastrophically. The 1,500 tonnes of graphite in the reactor core caught fire and began spewing radioactive particles and debris across the countryside. The inferno proved impossible to control. The radioactive plume rose several thousand feet, drifting across eastern and northern Europe over the following days, even reaching North America.

Why?

The facts are quite extraordinary, revealing poor planning, incompetence, lack of clear instructions, and recklessness as to risk assessment.

Managers wished to discover experimentally on Reactor 4 whether, in the event of a total loss of electrical supply to the plant, and therefore to the emergency control systems, the RBMK type reactor's cooling system would continue running properly and keep it safely under control until supply was restored. The cooling system would rely on the steam turbines continuing to rotate to generate sufficient electricity for this purpose. Incredibly, the reactor's emergency control systems were disabled to ensure that the conditions for the experiment were realistic.

The experiment was intended to be carried out by the day shift but the start was delayed because of problems occurring elsewhere on the plant that day. Yet the temporarily appointed chief engineer decided to go ahead.

A shift change during the evening meant that incoming night workers who had not been properly briefed now took over the experiment. The seeds of disaster had now been sown.

The design of the RBMK reactor also contributed to the accident. The characteristics of the coolant (water) were such that under certain circumstances neutron production, and thus heat, could spiral out of control and cause a steam explosion. The conditions required for the test carried out on 26 April resulted in the plant being operated in this dangerous condition.

What happened next?

A series of operational errors during the night caused the rate of reaction to increase. The temperature within the reactor core began to rise. The ill-prepared workers, confused by operating manuals that had been amended many times, discovered that they were not sure how to control the reactor's behaviour without using the emergency controls. Nevertheless the experiment continued. By the time a decision was taken to reactivate the controls manually it was too late. By then the heat had damaged vital components and the reaction was now out of control. Minutes later, a colossal steam explosion blew the top off the reactor.

On 27 and 28 April monitors in Sweden and Finland picked up heightened levels of radioactivity. At first a problem was suspected at a Swedish nuclear plant. The Russians did not admit to the event until the evening of 28 April. Later the event was to be classified as Level 7 on the International Nuclear Event Scale, the only nuclear incident ever to have been 'awarded' this level of severity. Estimates have put the amount of radioactive fallout from the explosion and fire at around 30 times the amount released in the bombing of Hiroshima and Nagasaki.

Some of the so-called 'liquidators' who cleaned up after the Chernobyl explosion, 1986.
Ukrainian National Chernobyl Museum

The principal radioactive pollutants released by the explosion were of three kinds. Iodine-131 has a short half-life of only a few days, but is easily absorbed by the human body, especially in children, where it can cause thyroid cancer. Caesium-137 and strontium-90 still pollute the area today; they have half-lives of several decades and are now found in the plants of the area and the animals that eat them. Finally, some of the reactor's fuel and byproducts, including uranium and plutonium, have half-lives of thousands of years. The outside world will need to be shielded from the reactor's remains for centuries to come.

The Chernobyl nuclear plant is at Pripyat, not far from the Ukrainian capital, Kiev. Evacuation of the population in the vicinity of Chernobyl began within 36 hours. Some 67,000 people had to move away, including 50,000 evacuated from Pripyat, which has been abandoned ever since. It is only recently that a handful of people have been allowed to return to the 'zone of alienation'.

Accounts differ as to the immediate and subsequent loss of life and disease associated with the disaster and the extent and effects of environmental pollution. The secretive nature of the Communist regime involved did not help at the time. Many lives must surely have been lost among the army of 'liquidators' – workers and soldiers drafted in to fight the blaze and clean up the site over the following days and weeks. Many thousands are believed to have died subsequently. There can be no way of knowing precisely.

The funfair in Pripyat was scheduled to open on 1 May 1986 – it was never used, and the town has been abandoned ever since.
Alex Cameron

Reactor 4 was encased in a hastily constructed concrete sarcophagus. Twenty or more years later this is deteriorating and needs to be replaced. Although the other three reactors at Chernobyl have since been shut down, RBMK type reactors are still operating in the Russian Federation and eastern European countries. These units have undergone design modifications to reduce their dangerous uncontrollability at low power levels.

Lessons

A positive outcome of the Windscale fire was the establishment of the Nuclear Installations Inspectorate (NII) under the Nuclear Installations Act of 1969. This brought to an end the self-policing of the industry by the Atomic Energy Authority. These days regulatory control is exercised by the HSE's NII, principally through licensing and inspections of installations. The experience of other countries is closely monitored to enable lessons to be learnt and disseminated.

While a strict regulatory regime is no guarantee that mistakes will not still be made by plant operators, the regulation of nuclear safety in the UK since Windscale has been reassuringly tight, empowering the inspectors to license sites with conditions imposed that are tailored to the technology and local situation, while confronting operators with their responsibilities for controlling the risks.

Conditions will be attached to the licence by the Inspectorate, which may also exercise powers of approval, consent or direction. Without its say-so, nothing nuclear can be built, commissioned, operated, maintained or decommissioned.

But the licence holder always remains responsible for the safe operation of the plant and for ensuring that risks are reduced to 'as low as reasonably practicable' (ALARP). Operators must produce a fully documented safety case for their plant, which the NII will assess before being satisfied that a licence to operate may be issued. Their assessments will follow published Safety Assessment Principles (SAPs).

Licences are kept under review, bearing in mind the designed life of the plant. When a licensee wishes to carry on operating beyond this period, a periodical safety review (PSR) must be carried out by the licensee to the satisfaction of the NII, which may require modifications to meet latest standards for maintaining safety.

The UK's approach has not been developed in isolation. It has evolved over time in the wider context of international experience and standard setting, for example by the International Atomic Energy Agency (IAEA) and the Nuclear Energy Agency of the Organisation for Economic Co-operation and Development (OECD).

While there have been some minor episodes at British nuclear facilities requiring intervention by the regulator, there have been no serious incidents since the Windscale fire. With nuclear energy once again on the agenda as a solution to the problems of climate change, the need for best regulatory and operational practices to be followed in every aspirant nuclear country has never been greater.

Sources

Windscale
Wakeford R. The Windscale reactor accident – 50 years on. *Journal of Radiological Protection* 2007; 27: 211–215. www.iop.org/EJ/article/0952-4746/27/3/E02/jrp7_3_e02.pdf

Three Mile Island
Kemeny J G. *Report of the President's Commission on the accident at Three Mile Island.* Washington, DC: US Government, 1979. www.pddoc.com/tmi2/kemeny/index.htm

Chernobyl
Chornobylinterinform (Ukrainian government agency for Chernobyl information). www.chernobyl.info (in English)
Chornobylinterinform. *Imennya zori – Chornobyl'.* Kiev: Chornobylinterinform, 1996. In Ukrainian – probably the best book of pictures connected to the disaster
Hawkes N, Lean G, Leigh D, McKie R, Pringle P and Wilson A. *The worst accident in the world: Chernobyl, the end of the nuclear dream.* London: Pan, 1986

General
Health and Safety Executive. *The tolerability of risk from nuclear power stations.* London: HMSO, 1988. www.hse.gov.uk/nuclear/tolerability.pdf

Chapter 16: Trouble in store

A few years back the Inspectorate became concerned at the increasing scale on which certain very hazardous materials were being stored. It felt that this not only presented greater risks to the people employed on site but also that in some cases the facilities represented a potential hazard to the community.
(Bryan Harvey, HM Chief Inspector of Factories, Annual Report 1971)

Failures to keep highly flammable fuels and hazardous chemicals in bulk storage safely have resulted in several major catastrophes around the world. The consequences are usually very severe.

Feyzin, France, 1966

On 4 January 1966 a cloud of liquefied petroleum gas (LPG) escaped from a large propane storage sphere at Elf's Feyzin refinery adjacent to the A6 autoroute near Lyon in France, during an operation to drain off an aqueous layer from the sphere.

What happened and why?

A blockage caused by ice had occurred when a valve was opened. When it suddenly freed itself, liquid propane gushed out of the sphere uncontrolled, forming a highly flammable cloud that drifted across the autoroute. Passing traffic was stopped but the gas is believed to have been ignited nevertheless by a car. Flames ran back to the leaking sphere, which began to burn fiercely as gasifying liquid continued to pour from the valve.

What happened next?

Firefighters attended but were inexperienced in dealing with such a fire and failed to cool the surrounding gas storage spheres. The first now burst, killing one man and cutting through the supporting legs of an adjacent sphere, which toppled over. As it too became engulfed in the flames, its relief valve lifted and spewed out more liquid propane. This was repeated until altogether five spheres had been destroyed in the ensuing fires.

In all, 18 people were killed and 81 more were injured.

Lessons

The incident at Feyzin raised a number of questions about the design and operation of the spheres, lack of insulation to prevent icing, lack of drainage away from the storage spheres to a bunded area where the LPG might have burned harmlessly, delays in effecting emergency procedures and flaws in emergency planning. Lessons learned for design and operating procedures were subsequently incorporated into industry codes of practice.

Bulk Terminals, Chicago, USA, 1974

Flammable gases are obviously hazardous, but the storage of other less obviously dangerous chemicals can also have disastrous outcomes when things go wrong on site.

On 26 April 1974 a bizarre sequence of events occurred at the Bulk Terminals tank farm in Chicago, Illinois, involving the release of silicon tetrachloride, a non-flammable material.

What happened?

At around 12.30 pm an unusual sound alerted operators who then noticed fumes rising from the bunded area around a 3,300 cubic metre storage tank of silicon tetrachloride. A flexible coupling had burst on a pipe system leading to the tank, dislodging a three-inch pipe from the tank wall and allowing liquid silicon tetrachloride to erupt from the fracture. This formed a gas cloud containing hydrogen chloride, a severe irritant.

Why?

A pressure relief valve had been closed unintentionally on a pipe system leading to the tank, one of 78 storage tanks of similar or larger size holding various materials on the site.

What happened next?

A strange sequence of events now started to unfold. As there was no fire or risk of explosion the local fire service did not respond to the incident. The terminal operators sat waiting for the owners of the chemical in storage to come and deal with it. The Environmental Protection Agency arrived with lime to neutralise it, but – extraordinarily – were denied access. As the afternoon wore on, the ever-growing gas cloud had spread almost a mile, was up to a quarter of a mile wide and had climbed almost as high into the sky. Early on Saturday morning an attempt was made to blanket the flooded bund with foam, but this failed to control the vaporisation. Fuel oil was next poured in to it together with eight truckloads of lime that had at last been allowed onto the site. Mercifully the vaporisation from the liquid now began to diminish and during the day an attempt was made to pump the remaining silicon tetrachloride from the leaking tank to another.

By Sunday morning rain had begun to fall, containing sufficient hydrochloric acid from the gas cloud to corrode power lines and stop four pumps. Finally a complete power failure prevented any more pumping. As the bund had now become full to overflowing a pit was dug nearby to contain the continuing leakage. An attempt was made to seal the leak with quick drying cement but this failed.

Just before midnight on Monday, four days after the coupling had burst and initiated the event, the leak was finally sealed. It would still take another four days to empty the tank and it would be a fortnight before the irritant fumes dropped to tolerable levels. In the meantime one man had died from exposure to the gas, 160 were sufficiently affected to be sent to hospital and 16,000 people had been evacuated from the neighbourhood.

Lessons
The incident began with a simple plant failure that had not been anticipated. It soon escalated as unplanned desperate measures were undertaken to control the leak of toxic materials. Poor emergency planning led to a failure to engage properly with the emergency services. The off-site consequences of poor safety management were severe but could have been far worse.

Even so, the consequences of the Chicago incident were bad enough. Much worse were those of a disastrous explosion involving LPG in the crowded confines of Mexico City.

San Juan Ixhuatepec, Mexico City, 1984

What happened?
More than 500 people, mostly members of the public, were killed on 14 November when a large LPG terminal blew up at San Juan Ixhuatepec.

Why?
The LPG plant, owned by PEMEX, the Mexican state-owned oil and gas company, was supplied with gas by pipeline from three refineries many miles distant to meet the demand for domestic and industrial use of gas in the sprawling capital city. There were numerous large storage spheres and cylinders on the site, interconnected by pipework. That day, two large storage spheres had already been refilled and a third was pumped about half full when an eight-inch diameter pipe connecting one of these spheres to other storage vessels ruptured, releasing highly flammable LPG to the atmosphere.

What happened next?
As the gas escaped, the pipeline pressure dropped. This was picked up by plant operators working in the control room but for some minutes it was

unclear what had caused it. They had no gas detection equipment and no emergency shutdown action was taken. Meanwhile, out of their sight, the escaping gas, heavier than air, formed a low but ever widening cloud, hugging the ground and spreading over some 3,000 square yards. Within minutes it had drifted towards a flare stack, where it was inevitably ignited, exploding with ground-shaking force and damaging nearby plant and equipment, including the terminal's fire water system.

Fires now broke out in several places around the terminal as the stunned operators tried to respond with an emergency shutdown. This came far too late to save the plant. Although pumping had at last been stopped, a succession of massive explosions occurred over the next 90 minutes as every storage sphere and tank became engulfed in fire, bursting and releasing ever more gas.

The terminal was totally destroyed. Off-site damage was equally severe, with the enormous blasts devastating the surrounding densely occupied neighbourhood and killing innocent occupants and passers-by. Others tried to escape by car, causing traffic jams which impeded the arrival of the emergency services.

Lessons
The first and subsequent gas explosions were BLEVEs (boiling liquid evaporating vapour explosions). The size of the first cloud has been estimated at some 6,000 cubic metres before it exploded. This is an enormous volume of energy to be released and it is not surprising that the

consequences were so severe. There were a number of factors that made matters worse. There was no gas detection system on the plant. Had there been, it is likely that the operators would have shut the plant down in time to prevent the major release of gas that caused the initial BLEVE.

The design and layout of the plant was poor and implicated the main fire water system in the initial blast, preventing any effective firefighting. Water sprays on the storage vessels then proved inadequate for keeping them cool and failed to prevent the spread of fire from vessel to vessel. The absence of a gas detection system linked to an automatic shutdown was critical.

The catastrophic events at Feyzin, Chicago and Mexico City should remain a warning to every operator of fuel storage premises that the hazard associated with storing large inventories of highly flammable fuels such as LPG and petroleum, or materials that can form flammable or toxic gas clouds when released, is very high indeed. The measures needed to control the risk of explosion and fire should be of a commensurately high order – as the explosions at the Buncefield fuel storage depot were to remind us in the UK some 20 years later.

Sources

Feyzin

Failure Knowledge Database: 100 selected cases. Fire and explosion of LPG tanks at Feyzin, France. http://shippai.jst.go.jp/en/Detail?fn=2&id=CC1300001
Health and Safety Executive. Refinery fire at Feyzin, 4th January 1966. www.hse.gov.uk/COMAH/sragtech/casefeyzin66.htm

Chicago

Health and Safety Executive. Gas release at the bulk terminals complex, Chicago, Illinois, 26th April 1974. www.hse.gov.uk/COMAH/sragtech/casechicago74.htm

Mexico City

Health and Safety Executive. PEMEX LPG terminal, Mexico City, Mexico, 19th November 1984. www.hse.gov.uk/comah/sragtech/casepemex84.htm

Chapter 17: Buncefield oil storage depot

The UK's most severe onshore industrial explosion since Flixborough (and Europe's biggest in peacetime) occurred one winter weekend in 2005. Thankfully no one was killed but £1 billion-worth of damage and distress was caused by a simple, preventable mistake.

What happened?

Just after six o'clock in the morning on Sunday 11 December, the slumbering Home Counties were rudely awoken by an enormous explosion at a little-known location called Buncefield.

Later that day as I was returning to London from the West Country, I saw from about 50 miles away a heavy-looking, dirty smudge hanging over the eastern horizon. On the car radio the news was announcing that an oil storage depot was ablaze near Hemel Hempstead, Hertfordshire.

Miraculously, no one had been killed, though 43 people suffered injuries and hundreds of nearby commercial and residential properties were severely damaged. Several more explosions occurred and fires continued to break out and burn for five days, causing a section of the nearby M1 to be closed while a vast plume of black smoke drifted away to the south east.

There are 108 fuel storage installations in the UK, many of which are large enough to fall within the scope of the Control of Major Accident Hazard Regulations (COMAH), which implement the European Seveso Directives. Buncefield was the fifth largest, actually comprising three sites under different management. It was on the site operated by a joint venture between the French oil company Total and the American company Chevron, known as Hertfordshire Oil Storage Ltd, that the incident began, three miles away from the busy town of Hemel Hempstead.

The depot abuts a local industrial estate and residential areas; this is never the happiest of situations, but not uncommon in our congested island. The site had opened in 1968, when there were few buildings in the vicinity. Over the years since then, commercial and residential development had been allowed by planners to encroach ever closer.

A variety of flammable fuels, including petrol and aviation kerosene, was pumped in batches from refineries through pipelines into the depot's storage tanks. Road tankers would draw down quantities from these for onward delivery throughout the region. The 400 daily tanker loadings at Buncefield were supplying about 8 per cent of the UK's total daily fuel

The Buncefield oil
storage terminal,
11 December 2005.
*Chiltern Air Support
Unit*

needs, including 20 per cent of south east England's and half of Heathrow Airport's demand for aviation fuel.

One of the initial explosions was so massive (it reportedly registered 2.4 on the Richter scale) that the blast is reputed to have been heard as far away as Holland and Belgium. Most of the site was destroyed, including 23 large storage tanks which had contained various highly flammable fuels.

An emergency response under Gold Command was quickly established by the Hertfordshire police, who immediately involved Hertfordshire County

Council, Hertfordshire Fire Service, other emergency services, Dacorum Borough Council, the Environment Agency, the Health Protection Agency and the HSE. Two thousand people had to be evacuated from homes in the vicinity on the advice of the emergency services. Many would never be able to return to their homes, such was the destruction.

Why?

A batch of unleaded petrol began to be delivered by pipeline to Tank 912 earlier that morning. This was no ordinary forecourt filling operation; very high volumes of fuel were being pumped into the tank very rapidly. Through a faulty piece of equipment – the failure of a safety device designed to prevent overfilling – some 300 tonnes of petrol were allowed to overflow unnoticed from the tank, cascading down the sides and overtopping inadequate bunding (which also served as containment for adjacent tanks).

Witnesses later reported that before the first explosion occurred, a white mist was seen forming over the site from about 5.30 am onwards, gradually spreading towards its boundary. This vapour cloud was being formed by evaporating fuel. Eventually – and inevitably – it found a source of ignition and detonated with gigantic force. Other tanks were soon engulfed in the raging fire that followed, triggering further explosions and releasing ever more fuel to feed the inferno.

Liquid fuel draining from damaged bunds soon covered the surface of a lagoon intended to provide water on site for fighting; instead the fire service would have to use a nearby reservoir, with the Grand Union Canal held in reserve. It took 25 pumps and 1,000 firefighters 32 hours to bring the main fires under control, with small fires continuing to break out over the next five days. By then 23 tanks and their contents had been lost to the fires and the blasts had damaged buildings as far as five miles away.

What happened next?

The economic and social impacts of the disaster were severe. The industrial estate contained 630 businesses employing about 16,000 people, many of whom lived locally and lost their homes. Many businesses were severely disrupted, some of their premises being completely destroyed, and some were forced into liquidation; the East of England Development Agency estimated the cost to local businesses at £70 million. Some local roads were closed to the public for months. There was a temporary disruption of fuel supplies throughout the south east of England and for a period aviation fuel had to be rationed.

The environmental impact was surprisingly less severe. Contamination of soil and ground water, caused by fuel spillage from inadequate bunding and the foam and water which ran off during the firefighting operation, is still being monitored by the Environment Agency as toxic chemicals were involved in the fire. It is believed, however, that pollution from the fallout from the smoke plume was minimal, as this dispersed over a very wide area. Fortunately, drinking water was unaffected.

The damage to the economy, public concern for the welfare of the people who had been living and working close to the Buncefield site, and the importance to planning authorities, public safety and the fuel storage industry of ensuring that this could never happen again, required decisive political action. The Rt Hon Lord Newton of Braintree was appointed as the independent chair of a Major Incident Investigation Board (MIIB), charged with overseeing the progress of an investigation by the UK 'competent authority' under COMAH and producing a report, with recommendations.

Acting together as the joint competent authority, the HSE and the Environment Agency began their thorough and wide-ranging investigation. This became one of the lengthiest and most costly industrial safety investigations ever. Around £17 million and 83,000 staff hours later, after publishing several interim reports with recommendations, Lord Newton reported the MIIB's final conclusions on 11 December 2008, the third anniversary of the disaster.

Shortly afterwards, criminal proceedings were announced by the HSE and the EA against five defendants. At the time of writing, these have not been completed.

Lessons
The economic cost of this major incident has been estimated at around £1 billion, including likely compensation, disruption to aviation, and the cost of investigation.

Although the investigation itself was costly and protracted, it took account of the relevant features of disasters such as at Enschede in the Netherlands (see Chapter 2) and Toulouse in France (see Chapter 22). Its thoroughness has enabled advice and guidance given to planning authorities and operators to be comprehensively overhauled and brought up to date. Even so, the report admitted that the mechanism leading to the extraordinary 'overpressure' of the massive unconfined vapour cloud explosion is still not fully understood and further scientific work is in progress to try to determine this.

The MIIB addressed numerous specific recommendations to the fuel storage industry in its several interim reports, enabling the industry and the authorities to respond to them before receiving the final report. This was an unusually helpful inquiry process. For example, it was interesting to note that the findings reported in the MIIB's fifth interim report (dealing with the design and operation of fuel storage sites) closely matched those of the US investigation into the explosion and fires at BP's Texas City refinery, referring in particular to the need to pay attention to improving process safety, human factors and organisational culture.

It is interesting to find that the likelihood of a massive explosion at Buncefield had not been anticipated in any previous major hazard assessment of this substantial site by the operators or the authorities, in spite of the presence of very large inventories of highly flammable liquids. Similarly, it had not been foreseen at other fuel storage sites. A collective 'cognitive tunnel vision' seems to have applied.

The Buncefield disaster fell within the criteria for a major accident as defined by the Seveso Directives, under which the UK 'competent authority' is obliged to send its findings to the European Commission. The Environment Agency and the HSE sent their joint report to the Commission in February 2009, which should enable the Commission to disseminate the lessons learnt about better practice for fuel storage throughout the EU.

Firefighters blanket wrecked storage drums with foam. *Chiltern Air Support Unit*

Sources

Buncefield Investigation website, www.buncefieldinvestigation.gov.uk/index.htm (includes photographs, maps and reports)

Environment Agency. Buncefield fuel depot. www.environment-agency.gov.uk/homeandleisure/pollution/water/89141.aspx

Health and Safety Executive. Control of major accident hazards (COMAH). www.hse.gov.uk/COMAH/index.htm

Chapter 18: The price of coal

Oh, where are you going to, all you big steamers,
With England's own coal, up and down the salt seas?
(Rudyard Kipling, 1865–1936)

Britain's industrial revolution was fuelled by 'King Coal' for over two centuries. It came at a heavy price.

Shortly before the First World War was to shock society by taking so many soldiers' lives in a futile military conflict, it was considered normal that many ordinary workers were dying in the winning of coal. For example, 269 men had been killed at the Prince of Wales Colliery, Aberfan, Wales, on 11 September 1878. Nearly a century later, this ill-fated village became the scene of another appalling tragedy, described in Chapter 1.

Around the beginning of the 20th century the chances of a coal miner being killed were ten times that of a factory worker, at one in 1,000.

There were many ways to die in the coal mines. Health problems included debilitating diseases like pneumoconiosis and emphysema caused by the dusty conditions. As well as facing the risks of rock falls, flooding and being mangled by powerful machinery, the men working in many deep mines, and particularly those in Wales, were at risk from the release and possibly disastrous explosion of a gas commonly known as 'coal damp' (methane). By the end of the 19th century this was reasonably well understood as the cause of underground explosions, and had led to the development of Sir Humphrey Davy's safety lamp and the well-known practice of taking canaries down to the coal face. The birds were found to be much more sensitive than men to changes in the atmosphere during mining resulting from the release of the gas entrained in the rock, and there is no doubt that the birds saved many lives by giving early warning. Later, they would be replaced by gas-sensitive monitoring equipment, and improved powerful mechanical ventilation would drain the methane away, keeping the gas well below its explosive limits.

However, much less well understood for many years was the causation of the even more severe explosions that could occur underground, caused by the ignition of coal dust.

Senghenydd, South Wales, 1913
Such an explosion caused the worst ever Welsh mining disaster.

What happened?
Four hundred and thirty-nine miners were killed at Universal Colliery, Senghenydd, on 14 October 1913 in a massive explosion of coal dust that ripped through the mine. Senghenydd had already claimed 81 miners' lives in an explosion in May 1901. This time the whole mine was destroyed.

Anyone underground who survived the explosion would probably have been suffocated by 'after-damp', an unbreathable gas consisting mostly of carbon dioxide and nitrogen dioxide left after the explosion had consumed most of the oxygen in the atmosphere.

Why?
It was many years before it was realised that a methane explosion underground was likely to dislodge and then detonate a vast accumulation of fine, highly flammable coal dust. Dislodged from surfaces throughout the mine by the force of the primary event, and inevitably ignited by the flames, this dust would then provide the fuel for a far worse secondary explosion, with a very rapidly accelerating flame front advancing throughout the mine.

What happened next?
Research carried out at the Safety in Mines Research Establishment in Buxton, which would much later form part of the HSE, eventually demonstrated that stone dust, a cheap, non-flammable, inert material, if stored at points around a mine and instantly released into the atmosphere in the event of a primary explosion, would suppress a secondary explosion by interfering with the flame front. This discovery was to save many lives.

Gresford, North Wales, 1934
However, in spite of this new understanding, regrettably Senghenydd was not the last major disaster in the British coal mining industry. Another massive explosion was to occur, again in Wales, this time at Gresford Colliery near Wrexham, where on 22 September 1934, 266 miners were killed. Of these, 254 remain buried in the mine to this day, a wheel from the pit head winding gear standing above as their permanent memorial.

Gresford Colliery was one of the deepest Welsh coal mines, an old pit dating from the early Victorian era. It had two separate shafts, known as the Dennis and the Martin, both descending over 2,200 feet and about 150 feet apart. Over many years the workings had fanned out a good distance from the shafts. By the 1930s it was a large mine employing over 2,000 men, but it had not yet been greatly mechanised.

Rescuers leave the
Gresford pit,
22 September 1934.
Getty Images

What happened and why?

During the night shift on 22 September an explosion occurred at two o'clock in the morning, followed by a raging fire in the part of the mine served by the Dennis shaft, and a mile away from it. There were about 500 men underground in the Dennis and Martin sections at the time, about half in each side.

Heroic rescue attempts were made during the night by the Gresford men who were not on the shift and miners from neighbouring pits, who all rushed to help save the men trapped in the Dennis section. But the intensity of the fire, the lack of adequate firefighting equipment, and the toxic gases gathering below ground were preventing safe entry. Three gallant rescuers lost their lives in the attempt, overcome by poisonous fumes.

Firefighting continued for another day, until it was reluctantly concluded that there was no hope for the men below and that both shafts should be sealed to starve the fire of oxygen. Only 12 bodies were ever recovered.

The Dennis section of the mine was never reopened and the bodies of the victims were left sealed in the mine, which was to become their permanent grave.

Most of the miners who died that day were poisoned by carbon monoxide, according to the coroner's inquest. Only six men managed to escape to safety, incredibly by climbing a ladder all the way from the pit bottom, almost half a mile below ground.

What happened next?

As was customary by now in the wake of a major disaster, an official inquiry opened on 25 October 1934. The dead miners were represented by Sir Stafford Cripps, who was later to become Chancellor of the Exchequer in the postwar Labour government.

The inquiry found that there had been management failures, a lack of safety measures, bad working practices, and poor ventilation in the pit. Prosecution followed in 1937, taken at Wrexham court against the pit manager, the under-manager and the United & Westminster Collieries Limited, the owners of the mine. The court found them guilty only of inadequate record-keeping.

Lessons

When I took charge of the HSE's several Inspectorates in 1989, my colleague, the late Mike Jones, then HM Chief Inspector of Mines, lent me a tape of a BBC radio programme made about the inquiry, telling me that it was essential listening for every mines inspector and that I would find it compelling and instructive. It certainly was. This was his way of reminding me of the heavy responsibility that I had just assumed for maintaining an effective Mines Inspectorate. I would not be allowed to forget it.

Bilsthorpe, England, 1993

Ironically, as the coal industry in Great Britain continued its inexorable decline in the closing decades of the 20th century, the safety culture that now existed in British mines had never been stronger and serious accidents were increasingly rare. However, any comfort to be gained from this was to be lost when three miners were killed underground in a single incident in 1993.

What happened?

The men were crushed to death at Bilsthorpe Colliery, Nottinghamshire, when a massive fall of rock brought down the roof of an underground roadway.

While the death toll was low compared with the disasters of the past, this tragic incident provoked a furious outcry from the mining unions and experts about the system of roof support that had been introduced at Bilsthorpe and elsewhere.

Why?

Traditionally, the roofs of underground roadways and galleries in British coal mines had been supported by steel arches. That method was tried and tested and had the confidence of the workforce. However, it was not infallible and was expensive compared to rock bolting, a system that depended on drilling deep into the surrounding rock formations and cementing them together with cables or rods and resin to prevent movement and falls. This had become the preferred method in many American and Australian mines. It was now being introduced in some British mines in the face of very strong objections from mining trade unions and some experts who believed the system was less safe than the use of steel arches. (Other experts in favour of the technique strongly disagreed.)

It was naturally immediately suspected that the rock bolting system at Bilsthorpe had failed, precipitating the collapse.

What happened next?

The Health and Safety Commission had been consulting for some time on new regulations for modernising the management of safety in mines to replace the old system that existed under the Mines and Quarries Act 1954. These proposals were controversial. The government had announced its intention to privatise British Coal and the mining trade unions were suspicious of the motives of the Commission and the HSE's Mines Inspectorate. The unions had emerged weakened from the bitter industrial disputes of the 1980s and feared that safety was being compromised for the sake of cost-cutting in preparation for privatisation of the mines.

The Mines Inspectorate had participated in the rescue operation at Bilsthorpe, which saved three men who had been trapped. The Inspectorate immediately began an investigation, and swiftly reported. Though not entirely excluding the possibility of rock-bolting having contributed to the collapse, the investigation found that the rock fall had been so unusually massive that it would have overcome a steel arch system, had one been provided. In the now distrustful atmosphere existing between the mining unions and the authorities, these findings failed to satisfy the unions, which demanded an independent inquiry.

The Commission acceded to this request, appointing Professor Sir Bernard Crossland, an eminent Fellow of the Royal Academy of Engineering. His findings, essentially that an unforeseeable geographical fault in the rock formation had led to the collapse at Bilsthorpe that neither steel supports nor rock bolting could have prevented, brought to an end the debate surrounding the technical cause of the tragic event at Bilsthorpe.

Arguments over rock bolting and the proposals to reform mining safety legislation continued but the Management and Administration of Safety and Health at Mines Regulations passed into law later in 1993 after a judicial review.

Rock bolting has since continued to be employed in some of the few remaining British deep mines. Thankfully there have been no more incidents causing multiple loss of life underground. Individual fatalities sadly continue to occur for the usual variety of reasons. However, over the last four years fatal injuries have averaged less than one a year.

Some lessons do seem to have been learnt.

Sources

Senghenydd
Brown J H. *The Valley of the Shadow: An account of Britain's worst mining disaster, the Senghenydd explosion.* Port Talbot: Alun Books, 1981
Wilson M. The Senghenydd Explosion. *Your Family Tree*, September 2006: 28–30.
www.yourfamilytreemag.co.uk/resources/yft/YFT41case1.pdf

Gresford
Walker H, Brass J and Jones J. Reports on the explosion at Gresford Colliery. *Colliery Engineering*, March 1937. www.dmm-gallery.org.uk/colleng/3703-01.htm

General
Health and Safety at Work etc Act 1974.
Management and Administration of Safety and Health at Mines Regulations 1993
Mines and Quarries Act 1954

Chapter 19: Railways

Ever since 1830, when Sir William Huskisson MP was struck by George Stephenson's steam locomotive *Rocket* near Manchester and became the first documented person to die in a railway accident, the great economic benefits brought to us by the railways have been soured by catastrophes. Some, such as the disastrous collisions of trains taking Victorian mill workers on their annual holidays to Blackpool, soon led to great advances in braking, signalling and systems for safe working of trains. Railway safety slowly improved, generally by adopting technical solutions that reduce the human capacity for errors.

Clapham Junction, London, 1988

But in spite of this progress, even towards the end of the 20th century, major accidents on the railways were still giving cause for concern. This concern was heightened when, on 12 December 1988, 35 people were killed and hundreds injured in one of Britain's worst train accidents.

What happened and why?

The crash occurred in a cutting near Clapham Junction during the morning rush hour after the driver of a crowded train approaching its next signal saw it change unexpectedly from green to red, and of course stopped. While he was reporting this to the signalling centre, his train was struck from behind by another, travelling at full speed, having passed a 'wrong side' green signal. This was through no fault of its driver; the green should have been a red because the preceding train was now standing on the same section of track. The violent collision jolted the stationary train off its rails into the path of a third train approaching in the opposite direction. A fourth just managed to brake in time, narrowly avoiding the wreckage and yet more carnage.

The investigation revealed that the technical cause of the 'wrong side' signal failure was a short circuit caused by contact between a relay and a live wire that had been left hanging loose in the system during recent resignalling work. There were also some important underlying causes relating to human factors and unsafe systems of work.

What happened next?

An inquiry led by Sir Anthony Hidden QC exposed serious shortcomings in the installation, commissioning and maintenance of the signalling equipment, attributed to long hours and fatigue among maintenance staff working on safety-critical systems.

Lessons

Hidden made a number of recommendations, including placing restrictions on the hours worked by maintenance staff. New, tighter procedures for testing and commissioning signalling systems were introduced.

In the meantime, the government of the day had decided to transform the nationalised railway by privatisation. It also decided to reassure a sceptical travelling public by transferring responsibility for safety regulation to the independent Health and Safety Commission and Executive, which would advise the government on the early introduction of a new regulatory regime based on safety cases.

The technical knowledge and experience of the long-established Railway Inspectorate – now transferred to the HSE – was now combined with the diverse engineering and scientific expertise of the national safety regulator, a powerful force for change. The HSE soon found there were numerous safety problems besetting this venerable industry.

Crash worthiness

Several of the train crashes had exposed the lack of crash worthiness of the ageing rolling stock. In some collisions involving Mark 1 passenger carriages – described by some as a 'shed on a rigid chassis' – they became uncoupled, their chassis overrode each other and the carriages telescoped, usually with fatal consequences for travellers. Investment in better designed and constructed rolling stock would gradually phase out this problem but progress was painfully slow. Research was carried out by the HSE into a 'cup and ball' form of coupling which would prevent carriages overriding in a collision, but the industry was reluctant to adopt it, preferring to wait for the arrival of new rolling stock.

Slam doors

Another serious problem with older rolling stock arose because of the flawed design of door locking mechanisms. This had not changed since first invented by the Victorian railway engineers. The safety of the door mechanism relied upon the exiting passenger slamming the door so that it closed properly and engaged the locking mechanism. Electrically interlocked doors controlled by a guard, which passengers could not operate themselves, were for the future.

When the HSE became involved in the early 1990s, it was surprised to learn that every year about 20 people were falling to their deaths from moving trains through these so-called 'slam doors'. The industry believed that these victims were either suicidal or drunk and appeared to accept that there was little to be done about it. The new safety regulator took a different view: the penalty for drunkenness should surely not be a death sentence. Research carried out by the Health and Safety Laboratory at Sheffield soon established that in the absence of maintenance, a door could be slammed shut and held closed in its frame, but the lock, if rusted or dirty, would not always engage. A passenger leaning on the door of a fast-moving train could then make a very quick exit, usually fatal.

Shamed into this realisation, a complacent industry was forced to respond with a programme of improved maintenance. It soon produced with a fanfare its own prototype for an electrically interlocked door mechanism which gradually became the industry standard, though it would be many years before the last 'slam door' trains left the network entirely. Within a few years the numbers of fatalities caused by falling from trains had been reduced dramatically, probably saving 200 lives in a decade.

Trackside working

Another pointer to the unsatisfactory attitudes to safety in the industry of that era could be found in statistics which showed that about 20 workers were being run down by trains every year as they carried out trackside maintenance. Their systems of work were unsafe and had not moved on with the times. As speeds increased, trains could approach so fast that workers could not hear them coming until it was too late to leave the track; it was also often difficult to see them in time. Again, the HSE was taken aback to find that this annual carnage seemed to be accepted as the norm. Pressure was applied to introduce safer systems of work; soon the numbers of fatal incidents of this kind had been reduced to single figures and then even zero, probably saving another 200 lives.

Signals passed at danger

While safety was improving in certain directions, there remained some major problems to be solved. The ageing infrastructure was in need of a comprehensive overhaul but the costs involved were enormous. The industry itself was still in managerial turmoil and had been for a number of years since the privatisation of the grossly inefficient nationalised railway in 1994. Railtrack had replaced the old British Rail and was now responsible for controlling the national infrastructure, including track and signalling, while various train operating companies held franchises for the different routes and services.

One seemingly intractable problem with potentially catastrophic consequences was the phenomenon known as a 'signal passed at danger' by drivers, known in the industry as a SPAD. This was an alarmingly frequent occurrence, often without serious consequences but sometimes causing fatal collisions. Drivers would not do this deliberately – they would be the first to die – but there were a number of human factor reasons which led even the most experienced drivers to make mistakes.

Together with my railway inspectorate colleagues in the HSE, I took this problem very seriously. Before the HSE became responsible for regulating railway safety, I had been fortunate to survive a collision between the southbound Liverpool to London express on which I was a passenger and a stationary northbound train at Colwich Junction, near Stafford, in 1986. Sadly, our driver was killed and a number of passengers were injured. The northbound train had passed a signal at danger and come to a halt in our path, straddling points which would have taken it on towards Manchester. Our train rounded the bend at 100 mph and there was no chance at all of avoiding the crash.

Alarmingly, when the HSE became more closely involved, we found that in the absence of a train protection system which would bring trains to a halt if drivers ran past a red light – never deliberately but for a variety of possible reasons – SPADs were a common occurrence. Several hundred were reported every year and inquiry after inquiry had recommended installation of an automatic train protection system (ATP). Such a recommendation had been made again after the crash at Colwich Junction.

The destroyed cab of one of the trains involved in the Colwich Junction crash, 19 September 1986.
Paul Miller

The long overdue investment in the infrastructure was at last beginning, but the industry's view was that ATP was unaffordable and that investment in a major revamp of the national signalling network would have to wait until new, less expensive technology became available. But disquiet with this policy would intensify after two more disasters occurred in quick succession.

The collision at Southall, London, 1997

On 19 September 1997, seven people were killed when an InterCity 125 express train coming from the West Country piled into a goods train carrying stone that was crossing the main line, having been properly signalled to do so. The driver of the InterCity train had passed a signal at danger while rummaging in his bag in preparation for arrival at the Paddington terminus.

The government appointed Professor John Uff to carry out an inquiry, which was still sitting when an even more shocking catastrophe occurred on the same line.

The collision at Ladbroke Grove, London, 1999

On a sunny October morning in 1999 one of the worst rail disasters in recent memory occurred on the Great Western Railway at Ladbroke Grove, just outside Paddington Station, London. Coming after a string of other serious incidents, it was to mark a long overdue turning point in the industry's attitude towards safety.

What happened?

On 5 October, not far from Paddington Station, the 8.06 am outward-bound Thames Trains service to Newbury and Bedwyn collided head-on with the approaching 6.03 am InterCity 125 express from Cheltenham, at a combined speed of 135 mph. The explosive sound of the impact was heard right across the capital, followed by the sight of a rising pall of black smoke as diesel fuel ignited and the two locomotives and the leading carriages caught fire. Emergency workers rushing to the scene were greeted by a ghastly sight of tangled, blazing wreckage.

Many lives were at first believed to have been lost in the InterCity's leading coach H, which was reduced to ashes. This proved not to be the case, but even so 31 people were killed and 227 hospitalised, with another 296 being treated on site for minor injuries.

Why?

The recently qualified and still inexperienced driver of the Thames Trains service had passed a signal (Signal 109) at danger. Bizarrely, the points then directed his train onto the main line, into the path of the

The remains of Coach H of the Great Western train involved in the Ladbroke Grove crash, 5 October 1999.
© *Metropolitan Police Authority*

oncoming express. Had his train simply been allowed to proceed on its own track, parallel to the InterCity's, the collision could not have occurred in spite of the driver's mistake. Sadly, he was among the many to die that morning.

He was not the first to have passed Signal 109 at danger. The Railway Inspectorate had been pressing Railtrack for improvements since an earlier SPAD had caused a near collision, but the signalling at Ladbroke Grove remained confusing. Signal 109 was not easy to pick out because of the clutter of equipment mounted on the overhead gantry, with several other signal lights serving a number of tracks, including the recently completed Heathrow Express line into Paddington.

What happened next?
The government, anticipating angry demands for a public inquiry, appointed Lord Cullen, veteran of the Piper Alpha inquiry, to lead it. In the event, two inquiries took place, one into the causes of the collision and the other looking into the wider issue of Automatic Train Protection, combining with Professor Uff's inquiry into the Southall collision.

Lord Cullen's report highlighted numerous contributory factors, such as Thames Trains' inadequate driver training procedures and Railtrack's failure to deal adequately with the visibility problems at Signal 109 even though there had been no fewer than eight reported SPADs at that signal in the previous six years.

The absence of 'flank protection' to divert the Thames Trains service onto a parallel line instead of the main line was criticised, as was Railtrack's Slough Signalling Centre's failure to send an emergency message by radio to the trains warning them to stop after they had realised that the Thames Train had passed Signal 109 at danger. The inspection procedures of the HSE's Railway Inspectorate did not escape criticism, either. Lord Cullen's numerous recommendations led, among other things, to the establishment of a Rail Safety and Standards Board in 2003 that would be independent of the industry, replacing a function previously performed within Railtrack.

In 2004 Thames Trains pleaded guilty to breaches of health and safety law associated with the incident and was fined a then record £2 million. The successor to Railtrack, Network Rail, was similarly prosecuted and paid a fine of £4 million in 2006.

The Railway Safety Regulations of 1999 required the fitting of a Train Protection Warning System (TPWS) to all passenger lines by 2003. In response Network Rail introduced TPWS across the entire network at a cost of £585 million. It was a giant step forward for railway safety.

However, in the meantime the industry had been lobbying ministers to reduce the number of regulatory bodies that it had to respond to. Responsibility for regulating safety on the railways had been transferred to the HSE just before privatisation. In his report on the disaster at Ladbroke Grove, Lord Cullen had recommended that the HSE should remain responsible for railway safety, but in 2006, flying in the face of the landmark principles established by the Piper Alpha inquiry, ministers acceded to the railway industry's demands. Responsibility for safety regulation and the Railway Inspectorate were transferred to the industry's economic regulator, the Office for Rail Regulation (ORR). A separate independent Rail Accident Investigation Branch was established along the lines of the Department of Transport's Air Accident Investigation Branch, focusing solely on rail safety improvements without laying blame or pursuing prosecutions.

Time will tell whether these were wise decisions.

Lessons

Faced with the industry's objections to the high cost of Automatic Train Protection and insufficient political backing, the safety regulator had been unable to force the pace of change. The 'nuclear option' – closing the railway – was of course simply not available. It took a major disaster, Ladbroke Grove, to act as the catalyst. As TPWS has demonstrated, technology can protect against the human capacity for making mistakes.

Sources

Clapham Junction
1988: 35 dead in Clapham rail collision. BBC News Online: On this day, 12 December. http://news.bbc.co.uk/onthisday/hi/dates/stories/december/12/newsid_2547000/2547561.stm
Hidden A. *Investigation into the Clapham Junction railway accident*. London: HMSO, 1989. www.railwaysarchive.co.uk/documents/DoT_Hidden001.pdf

Colwich Junction
Olver P M. *Report on the collision that occurred on 19 September 1986 at Colwich Junction in the London Midland Region, British Railways*. London: HMSO, 1988
Rail crash remembered 20 years on. BBC News Online, 13 September 2006. http://news.bbc.co.uk/1/hi/england/staffordshire/5338662.stm

Southall
1997: Six dead in Southall train disaster. BBC News Online: On this day, 19 September. http://news.bbc.co.uk/onthisday/hi/dates/stories/september/19/newsid_2524000/2524283.stm

Uff J. *The Southall Rail Accident Inquiry report*. London: HMSO, 2000.
www.railwaysarchive.co.uk/documents/HSE_Southall1997.pdf

Ladbroke Grove
Lord Cullen. *The Ladbroke Grove Rail Inquiry report: parts 1 and 2*. Sudbury: HSE
Books, 2001
Paddington remembered 10 years on. BBC News Online, 5 October 2009.
http://news.bbc.co.uk/1/hi/england/london/8290166.stm

Chapter 20: Crowd crushes

Anyone who has been carried along off their feet by the sheer force of a packed, fast-moving crowd will have experienced the fear that if they fell they would be unable to get up again – ever. This fear is well justified, as many disasters show.

Bethnal Green, London, 1943

During the Second World War, more people died in the crowd crush that took place at an East End Underground station than in the Silvertown factory explosion of the First World War (see Chapter 9). It was the worst civilian disaster of the war.

What happened and why?

In 1943 the Bethnal Green Underground station in east London had not yet come into service as a railway station. But its platforms were deep underground and the station had come to be used by local residents as a shelter from the air raids. It had the capacity to hold up to 7,000 people and thousands would often safely spend the night there during the London Blitz.

At about a quarter past eight in the evening of 3 March 1943 the air raid sirens began to sound, warning of yet another German bombing raid. Soon there were hundreds of people hurrying into the station during the blackout as they had done many times before during a raid.

But this time it was different. As hundreds ran into the entrance and down the stairs to safety, a battery of anti-aircraft rockets recently installed in a nearby park opened up suddenly, panicking the crowds that were still scurrying in for shelter. A woman carrying a small child tripped and fell as she hurried down the narrow stairway. Scores of people rushing down behind her then fell on top of each other as more people hurried in above, unaware of what had happened.

A hundred and seventy-three people died in the crush, including 62 children.

What happened next?

As it was wartime, the government refused to hold a public inquiry, fearing that its findings would damage morale, but years after the war had ended a report of a secret investigation carried out for the government by a Mr Laurence Dunne was disclosed. It was too late to make any useful recommendations.

Pilgrims perform the Tawaf (circumambulation of the Kaaba) during the Hajj.
Muhammad Mahdi Karim

The Hajj, Mecca, Saudi Arabia

Over the years, the Hajj, the annual pilgrimage of Muslims to the Holy City of Mecca, has been sadly blighted by incidents involving crowd crushes, often during the ritual stoning of the Devil. The sheer numbers involved almost defy management of their safety – literally millions arrive during the festival.

The accident statistics beggar belief. An appalling accident occurred in 1990 when over 1,400 pilgrims died in a stampede inside a pedestrian tunnel leading from Mecca towards Mina and the Plains of Arafat. In 1994, 270 people died in a stampede at the stoning of the Devil, and 118 pilgrims were killed in a crushing incident on the Jamarat Bridge in 1998. In 2001, 35 pilgrims were trampled to death in a stampede during the stoning ritual at Mina; in 2004, 251 were killed and 244 injured in yet another stampede; and in 2006, 346 were killed and 289 injured in a crowd crushing accident at the Jamarat Bridge.

The huge numbers of people – hundreds of thousands at a time – who come to the site of the stoning of the Devil have to cross the Jamarat Bridge to reach it. As they jostle for position it is easy for someone to trip and fall, causing a domino effect and lethal crush behind them.

Steps have been taken to try to prevent these disasters in future and the bridge is being modified to include five separate levels and access routes to improve the flow of people.

In 2009, thanks to these improvements, no one died in a crowd stampede. We have not suffered such extreme events in the UK but we should be careful to note events abroad from which we can learn and improve things here. Global statistics are not easy to come by but it is thought that at least 2,000 people have been killed in accidents involving crowds during the last decade alone.

Managing the human factor in crowd behaviour will always be challenging. Individuals in a crowded environment do not behave like members of a trained workforce who are familiar with their surroundings and the attendant hazards. Solving crowd safety problems often require solutions that are unique to the site in which they occur.

The Pinner Fair, London

An example is the Pinner Fair. While it might seem a minuscule event compared with the scale of the Hajj, several years ago concerns were raised over the potential for a serious crowding incident at the fair. It had been held annually since the 14th century under an ancient charter in the narrow High Street of this Middlesex village. But as time went on, it had changed in character from a country hiring fair with entertainers and a market atmosphere to a full scale funfair with large dynamic rides. The fair's popularity and profitability had become so great that numerous ride operators were travelling from afar to set up ever more exciting attractions, spilling into the side streets and attracting huge numbers of revellers, young and old.

The problem to be solved was primarily not one of public order but of public safety. If an accident occurred, whether by crushing or by the failure of a ride, it seemed unlikely that the emergency services could get through the crowds to the scene.

An assessment of risks at the fair was commissioned from the HSE's Health and Safety Laboratory, which had already done work to assist the investigation and public inquiry into the Hillsborough crowd disaster. Their report laid the foundation for a number of improvements to the fair's layout and organisation which have enabled it to carry on into the 21st century, to the continued benefit of the operators and enjoyment of the public.

Lessons

The HSE also commissioned research in 1991 to study crowd behaviour, the different management and control methods currently in use, and the effect of crowd size, flows and venue design on the potential for overcrowding. This led to the publication of guidance called *Managing crowds safely*, setting out some key points to consider during risk assessment. In 1998 the HSE published further research into a risk assessment methodology for crowd safety.

An adequate risk assessment, though vital, is of course only one step towards safe operation in any situation involving large crowds, whether inside a stadium or outside at a fairground or pop concert. Sound operational plans that specify control measures and describe the system for managing the risks, identifying key people, their responsibilities and arrangements for training staff, will need to be prepared and regularly reviewed with the emergency services.

Given the crowd catastrophes that have occurred around the world, we cannot afford to disregard these lessons.

Sources

Bethnal Green
The Bethnal Green Tube disaster 1943. www.barryoneoff.co.uk/html/tube_disaster.html
WW2 People's War: The Bethnal Green Tube shelter disaster. BBC History. www.bbc.co.uk/ww2peopleswar/stories/09/a795909.shtml

The Hajj
Hundreds killed in Hajj stampede. BBC News Online, 12 January 2006. http://news.bbc.co.uk/1/hi/world/middle_east/4606002.stm
Incidents during the Hajj. Wikipedia, http://en.wikipedia.org/wiki/Incidents_during_the_Hajj

Pinner Fair
Pinner Fair 2009 website, www.pinnerlocal.co.uk/Company.aspx?cid=5342

General
Health and Safety Executive. *Managing crowds safely* (INDG142). www.hse.gov.uk/pubns/indg142.htm.

Chapter 21: Stadium tragedies

Many horrific disasters have occurred in crowding situations involving football fans in the UK and abroad. It has taken a century for the lessons to be properly learnt and applied and finally took the deaths of 96 fans in the worst ever British football disaster to galvanise the authorities into determined action.

But first, a look at the slow and painful learning process that has cost so many lives.

Ibrox Park, Glasgow, 1902

On 6 April 1902 a crowd of 80,000 packed Glasgow Rangers' Ibrox Park football ground to watch Scotland play England. During the match, an area of recently erected wooden terracing supported by a steel frame suddenly collapsed, taking hundreds of spectators with it in a tangle of broken timbers and twisted steel. Twenty-five people were killed and over 500 were seriously injured.

This faulty design and inadequate construction of terracing was subsequently replaced voluntarily at many grounds by terracing supported on reinforced concrete. Remarkably, considering the tight regulation and licensing that had already been imposed on other places of mass entertainment such as music halls and theatres, the authorities took no initiative after the disaster to regulate the safety of football grounds, perhaps fearing they would assume liability. In fact, in spite of the many injuries to spectators and near misses that continued to occur, football would be allowed to regulate itself for the best part of the 20th century.

Wembley Stadium, London, 1923

A near-disaster occurred in 1923 at the first FA Cup Final to be played at the new Wembley Stadium. It had been built with a capacity for 127,000 spectators, a very large number, but a huge crowd of 300,000 people had come in hope of admission and were trying to enter the ground. The pitch was invaded before the match began but legend has it that a policeman riding a white horse managed to restore order. Miraculously, no one was seriously hurt. From then on the most important fixtures were made all-ticket only, which avoided these phenomenal numbers arriving at the gates.

Burnden Park, Bolton, England, 1946

Tragically, there was no near-miss at an overcrowded Burnden Park, home of Bolton Wanderers, after the war.

Bodies of victims of
the crush at Burnden
Park in Bolton,
9 March 1946.
Getty Images

What happened and why?

During an FA Cup quarter-final between Bolton Wanderers and Stoke City, attended by 85,000 who had packed themselves into the ground, 33 supporters were crushed in the crowd and asphyxiated.

What happened next?

An inquiry was held under Moelwyn Hughes, who recommended that the size of football crowds should be limited. But little happened to improve safety at football grounds until 1971, when tragedy returned to Ibrox Park.

Ibrox Park, Glasgow, 1971

On 2 January, towards the end of an Old Firm match between Rangers and Glasgow Celtic, many fans had begun to leave down a stairway, thinking the game was all but over, when it is thought a roar from the crowd at a final goal caused some to turn back, obstructing those who were following. The sheer numbers and weight of people filling the stairway caused a terrible mêlée, in which 66 fans, including many children, were crushed to death. Over 200 were seriously injured.

The same stairway had already been a factor in previous accidents. An inquiry into the disaster was soon followed by the passing of the Safety of Sports Grounds Act 1975, which put a duty on local councils to inspect and issue safety certificates at sporting facilities.

Ibrox was rebuilt, with seating for all fans and improved exits. But this was still exceptional. In 1985 a disastrous fire in Bradford showed that much more needed to be done to improve safety at football grounds.

The Bradford City FC fire, England, 1985

I had just returned to my flat in Liverpool one Saturday afternoon when the telephone rang. It was an inspector at the Leeds office of the HSE, phoning from his home: "Is your television on? You need to see this." As my set warmed up, a truly horrific scene unfolded before my eyes.

What happened?

Bradford FC had already won promotion that season to the Second Division when the end of season match against Lincoln City started on Saturday 11 May 1985. The stadium was crammed with celebrating fans. The game was only a few minutes old when the grandstand caught fire, with flames spreading rapidly to adjoining parts of the wooden structure. Fifty-six supporters died that afternoon from burns or smoke inhalation. Hundreds were injured.

Why?

Combustible rubbish dropped by spectators had been allowed to accumulate for many years under the 77-year-old wooden stand. The club had been advised to remove this but had not done so.

The fire at Bradford FC, 11 May 1985. *Getty Images*

What happened next?

The rubbish was probably ignited by a carelessly discarded cigarette dropping through a gap in the boards. The wooden stand caught alight in G Block and fire spread rapidly, accelerated by hot bitumen dripping from the ancient roof. The entire stand was ablaze within minutes. Many fans then became trapped in a crush behind doors at the back of the stand as they tried to get away from the choking smoke and flames. They died from smoke inhalation where they stood, unable to escape through the doors (because they opened inwards) and unable because of the crush to flee to the safety of the open pitch below.

Nor did it help that the turnstiles had been locked earlier to prevent unticketed access. However, many fans were saved from the blaze by the heroic efforts of friends and the police.

Lessons

A public inquiry was held in Bradford Town Hall by Mr Justice Popplewell to investigate the disaster and make recommendations. The principal outcome was to ban the construction of new wooden grandstands at football grounds.

The club had been unable to afford to replace the old wooden stand but it was clearly negligent to have allowed so much combustible rubbish to accumulate beneath it.

There was no prosecution, though the authorities involved later faced a civil action for compensation from the victims. The Popplewell inquiry's recommendations would eventually lead to the introduction of new legislation to improve safety at football grounds, the Fire Safety and Safety at Places of Sports Act 1987 and the Safety of Sports Grounds Regulations 1987. Wooden stands were outlawed.

The Heysel Stadium disaster, Brussels, 1985

In the meantime another horrific crushing disaster occurred in Belgium that would blight the international reputation of English football for years to come. 1985 was turning out to be a very bad year indeed.

What happened and why?

A fracas between rival fans at a European Cup final between Liverpool and Juventus held at the Heysel Stadium in Brussels led to Juventus supporters panicking as they attempted to escape, pressing against a wall that suddenly collapsed around them. Thirty-nine were trampled and crushed to death and more than 350 were injured.

What happened next?
Riot police arrived to restore order while emergency services struggled to
help injured survivors. Incredibly, the match was allowed to continue, the
police believing there would be worse trouble if it were stopped.

As a result of the riot, for which supporters of the English side were
blamed, all English clubs were banned from European football for five
years. Fourteen Liverpool supporters were eventually convicted of
involuntary manslaughter and sentenced to three years' imprisonment.

But worse was still to come.

The Hillsborough stadium disaster, Sheffield, England, 1989

On 15 April 1989 Sheffield Wednesday's ground at Hillsborough,
Sheffield, was packed for an FA Cup semi-final between Liverpool and
Nottingham Forest.

What happened and why?
Huge numbers of supporters were still arriving at the gates as the match
started, with Liverpool fans being shepherded through the turnstiles into
two narrow pens separated by barriers at one end of the ground. As the
growing numbers pressed behind them, supporters trying to enter the
ground had no idea what was happening ahead of them and continued to
push their way in. By now those at the front of the pens were being
crushed against the wire fencing which prevented them from escaping onto
the pitch.

Outside, the police were struggling to cope with the numbers of arrivals
and remained unaware of the disaster looming in the crowded pens.
Concerned about the safety of the swelling crowd surging in front of the
turnstiles, they decided to open another gate. It proved to be a fatal error,
allowing a flood of people to rush into the tunnel behind the pens, adding
their weight to the chaotic crush. By now the fans pressed against the
front of the pens were fighting for their lives. The match was abandoned
after six minutes but by then 94 Liverpool supporters had been
asphyxiated or crushed to death. Over 750 were injured, many very
seriously, and two more would die later.

What happened next?
An inquiry into this appalling disaster was set up within a month, led by
Lord Justice Taylor, whose report identified the principal cause as a
failure of the police to control the crowds. In addition to that, a
combination of factors had combined to cause the catastrophe. There
were problems related to the wire fencing and steel barriers against which

Flowers and scarves left in memory of the victims at Hillsborough, 1989.
Getty Images

many had been fatally crushed. The fencing had been installed to prevent pitch invasions and hooliganism. There had been communication failures between officials on the inside and those outside, and incredibly when ambulances arrived for the injured only one was allowed onto the pitch, and then it retreated.

The Taylor report led to millions of pounds being spent on the conversion of football grounds to all-seater stadiums and the removal of barriers at the front of stands.

In 1993 the first new all-seater stadium to be built since the Taylor report opened at Millwall, and all new stadiums are now all-seater.

Lessons
Unlike theatres, cinemas and other places of mass public entertainment, football had been allowed to be self-regulating for far too long.

Sources

Ibrox Park 1902
Shiels R S. The fatalities at the Ibrox disaster of 1902. *Sports Historian* 1998; 18 (2): 148–155. www.aafla.org/SportsLibrary/SportsHistorian/1998/sh182k.pdf

Wembley
Football History. The 1923 FA Cup. www.footballhistory.eslreading.org/facup/page63/page63.html

Burnden Park

Bolton Revisited. Burnden Park disaster 1946. www.boltonrevisited.org.uk/s-burnden-disaster.html

Crowd Dynamics. British football disasters. www.crowddynamics.co.uk/Disasters/british_football_disasters.htm (this link also has information on the Ibrox Park (1971) and Bradford incidents)

Ibrox Park 1971

1971: Sixty-six die in Scottish football disaster. BBC News Online: On this day, 2 January. http://news.bbc.co.uk/onthisday/hi/dates/stories/january/2/newsid_2478000/2478305.stm

Bradford City

Firth P. *Four minutes to hell: the story of the Bradford City fire*. Manchester: Parrs Wood, 2005

Footballclips.net. Bradford City Football Club fire – May 11th, 1985 (video footage of the disaster – includes disturbing scenes). www.footballclips.net/forum/general-video-clips/3760-bradford-city-football-club-fire-may-11-1985-warning-clip-may-offend.html

University of Bradford. The papers of the Popplewell Inquiry into crowd safety at sports grounds. www.brad.ac.uk/library/special/popplewell.php

Heysel Stadium

Juve Liverpool – 29 maggio 1985 – tragedia Heysel (Italian footage of the disaster). www.youtube.com/watch?v=0LWDfV-CebI

The Heysel disaster. BBC News Online, 29 May 2000. news.bbc.co.uk/1/hi/uk/768380.stm

Hillsborough

Hillsborough Justice Campaign website, www.contrast.org/hillsborough

Sheffield City Council. Hillsborough disaster bibliography. www.sheffield.gov.uk/sys_upl/templates/AssetBrowser/AssetBrowser_disp.asp?ItemID=21461&basketPage=&basketItem=&pgid=128790&tid=186&page=2

Chapter 22: The human factor

The human factor should never be overlooked. People make mistakes, usually because of organisational weaknesses or failures of the systems within which they have to work. The interfaces between people and the hazards to which they may be exposed, whether they arise from machines, the working environment or the pressures of the job, can be many and complex but they are nevertheless manageable. Failure to take them into account and manage the risks of harm the hazards present can lead to disaster, whereas good training, supervision and communication of information will lead to a competent workforce who can be relied on to identify hazards, foresee and manage risks, and cope well with the unexpected – in short, a robust safety culture. Unforeseen and unexpected events faced by a less than competent management or workforce are often the starting point for disaster, as we have already seen in earlier chapters and as we shall see again here.

Sometimes an 'act of God', such as a storm or earthquake, can be blamed for a disaster, but more often than not someone has played a part in its causation or has managed to make matters worse.

The major incident at the Texaco refinery, Milford Haven, South Wales, 1994

A severe electrical storm on the morning of Sunday 24 July 1994 was the beginning of a series of events that knocked out 10 per cent of the UK's oil refining capability for several months.

What happened?

A lightning strike during the storm started a fire that caused the crude distillation unit that provided feed to the Pembroke Cracking Company (PCC) units to be shut down. Knock-on effects during the morning required all PCC units to be shut down but the fluidised catalytic cracking unit (FCCU) was kept running. About five hours later, an explosion occurred at the FCCU, followed by fires that also affected the vacuum distillation, alkylation and butamer units.

Why?

While the sequence of events began with the fire caused by the lightning strike, causing a plant upset to which operators attempted to respond, unfortunately matters were made worse in an attempt to keep the plant running. A potentially deadly combination of failures in management, equipment and control systems coincided, leading to flammable hydrocarbons being continuously pumped into a process vessel where a malfunctioning valve prevented their exit. Once the vessel was full, the hydrocarbon liquid could only escape through the pressure relief system and then to the flare line.

The flare system was not designed to cope with this abnormal operation. The flammable liquid burst through the FCCU flare knock-out drum and caused a failure in the outlet pipe, releasing 20 tonnes of hydrocarbon liquid and vapour which found a source of ignition 100 metres away and exploded.

What happened next?
The violent explosion caused a major hydrocarbon fire at the flare drum outlet and a number of secondary fires. Fortunately, these were contained by firefighters and escalation to the rest of the plant was avoided by cooling any nearby vessels that contained flammable liquids. It was then decided that as the explosion had knocked out the flare relief system, the safest course of action was to allow the fires to continue to burn. They were finally extinguished two days later.

The HSE mounted an investigation into this major incident, which could have had very serious consequences for personnel on and off site. Mercifully there had been no fatalities and few injuries. A supervisor broke his arm when he was blown off a gantry by the force of the explosion.

Later, the partner companies operating the refinery were fined £200,000 for breaches of health and safety law.

Lessons
There were several lessons to be learnt from this disaster:
- Human factors were in play: the control panel did not provide an overview of the whole process and an excessive number of alarms in the emergency situation reduced the effectiveness of operators to respond.
- A control valve was shut when the control system indicated it was open.
- The plant had been modified without an assessment of the potential consequences.
- Attempts were made to keep the unit running when it should have been shut down.

The fire at Windsor Castle, England, 1992
Not every disaster causes carnage, but disasters they still can be. Such was a recent fire at a royal residence. The Queen suffered her *annus horribilis*

in 1992, during which a fire at one of her royal homes became a national disaster.

Fortunately, in the end, it was only money; luckily no one died in bringing the blaze under control.

What happened and why?
On 20 November 1992 a devastating fire at Windsor Castle broke out in the Queen's Private Chapel while restoration work was in progress. A curtain was set on fire by the heat from a powerful lamp that a worker had left too close to it. Within minutes the fire had spread and was raging through the State Apartments.

What happened next?
The castle's own fire brigade tackled the blaze immediately but it was beyond their capacity to control. Minutes later the county brigade arrived with 10 appliances and set to; within an hour the numbers fighting the fire had built up to 39 appliances and 200 firefighters attending from London and surrounding counties. The blaze was brought under control within two hours, though by then the roof of the State Apartments was collapsing. Nine hours passed before the fire was fully extinguished.

The remains of St George's Hall, Windsor Castle, after the fire on 20 November 1992.
Tim Graham/ Getty Images

The response from the brigades had been magnificent. The fire was said to have attracted the largest firefighting operation in Greater London for 20 years.

Five firefighters were taken to hospital and the Surveyor of the Queen's Pictures is believed to have suffered a heart attack. A young decorator suffered burns while rescuing paintings. Fortunately, no one was killed, but the damage was extensive and very expensive to repair. Over 100 rooms and their contents were damaged.

What happened next?
The fire had added to the Queen's personal woes during that year, which she famously described in a speech as her *annus horribilis*. She contributed £2 million from her own pocket to the total repair bill, thought to be £40 million. To help recoup the cost, Buckingham Palace was opened to the public for the first time and a modest charge was introduced for entry there and to Windsor Castle. Repairs were not completed until 1997.

Lessons
It doesn't take much to start a big fire. Many a building has been burnt down by someone's careless use of a blowlamp or cutting torch. In this case the heat from a misplaced, powerful electric lamp was quite sufficient.

The water poisoning incident at Camelford, Cornwall, England, 1986
The UK's worst drinking water pollution and poisoning incident happened on 6 July 1988, when water supplied to some 20,000 residents of north Cornwall was accidentally contaminated with aluminium sulphate.

What happened and why?
The driver of a tanker delivering the chemical from Bristol had never been to the Lowermoor treatment plant near Camelford before. He had been given a key by another driver and was simply told that the aluminium sulphate tank could be found on the left, once he was inside the building. He found the key fitted a manhole cover at a tank on the left, removed it and mistakenly discharged his 20-tonne load of aluminium sulphate into the wrong tank – the one holding treated water for consumption.

In spite of complaints, it took nearly a week for the water authority to identify the cause of the contamination and warn its customers. Thousands of people had drunk the water by the time the mistake was discovered. Many subsequently complained of serious health problems.

What happened next?
In 1991 South West Water Authority was fined £10,000 at Exeter with £25,000 costs for supplying water likely to endanger public health. Three years later, 148 victims of the incident reached an out-of-court settlement, with payments ranging from £680 to £10,000.

There was no public inquiry. The water authority was later privatised by the government. Eventually, Michael Meacher MP, by then the Environment Minister, referred the matter to the Committee on Toxicity of Chemicals in Food, Consumer Products and the Environment for them to examine the concerns about health effects.

In 2007 a police investigation was ordered by the Coroner after two local women who had drunk the water died.

Lessons
It was the driver's mistake, but he had not been properly instructed and supervised. This was a grievous error by the company, in view of the high risk of a human error being made by someone making their first visit to the works, alone and unsupervised.

The explosion at the AZF factory, Toulouse, France, 2001
Terrorists were at first suspected when on 21 September 2001 a mighty explosion occurred at the AZF chemical works near Toulouse, France. But it was someone's error at the factory that had caused it.

What happened and why?
The entire factory was destroyed when 300 tonnes of ammonium nitrate in storage blew up. The terrifying explosion was heard 50 miles away and left an enormous crater 200 metres wide and 25 deep. Twenty-nine people were killed, including a child. Around 2,500 were seriously injured and many more suffered slight injuries, mainly cuts from flying glass as windows shattered in the neighbouring suburbs of Toulouse.

It was not a terrorist attack; the ammonium nitrate (AN) had been mistakenly placed and accidentally contaminated with other chemicals in the store, with which it reacted and then exploded.

What happened next?
The emergency services took the drastic step of evacuating 40,000 people from the surrounding neighbourhoods, schools and hospitals, fearing further explosions. None occurred but many people were made homeless for a number of days.

The Lycée Professionnel Gallieni school was badly damaged by the explosion at AZF Toulouse, 21 September 2001. *Anton Merlina-Bonnafous*

A government inquiry came to the conclusion that the AN had been stored improperly, due to another chemical, sodium dichloroisocyanate, being mistakenly placed in the store alongside it. This, they believed, had caused a reaction forming nitrogen dichloride, an unstable compound that had then heated and detonated the AN.

Lessons

The root cause of the disaster was attributable not so much to chemistry as to human error in allowing the ammonium nitrate to be stored at risk of contact with other chemicals, a well-known hazard with this material.

This was an exceptionally large blast because of the very large quantities in store, but fires and explosions involving AN are not uncommon. For example, on 14 October 1982 Cory's Warehouse in Ipswich, where large quantities of fertiliser materials were stored, had caught fire because of mixed storage of ammonium nitrate with potassium nitrate and compound fertilisers. No one was hurt as the emergency services rightly evacuated 2,000 people from the vicinity, fearing a huge explosion. Fortunately, no blast occurred, or the consequences for Ipswich could have been very severe, as the city of Toulouse discovered.

The cockling tragedy at Morecambe Bay, England, 2004

I was once flown across Morecambe Bay from the gas terminal at Barrow-in-Furness to Blackpool by helicopter and was struck by the eerily beautiful sight of the vast expanse of sands exposed by the falling tide. There was nothing to indicate the danger they presented to anyone venturing too far from the shoreline. But I remembered that in 1856 some young people seeking work had come to grief on their way to a hiring fair in Lancaster when they took a short cut across the sands. Unaware of the risk they were taking, they were all drowned, unable to outrun the incoming tide rushing across the sandflats.

What happened and why?

Unfortunately, they were not the last to underestimate the dangers of the Bay. On 5 February 2004, around nine o'clock in the evening, a dark, wintry night had fallen over these same sands as the tide began to turn. Local cocklers, who made their living by harvesting the abundant shellfish and knew every bank and channel like the backs of their hands, had already left the beach, shouting warnings to a group of Chinese men and women still raking the sands. Their warnings were unheard, unheeded or not understood by people from a faraway country, working for gangmasters who cared nothing for their safety.

Morecambe Bay at low tide.
Jason Dickie

Their fate was sealed by about half past nine. In the dark, suddenly aware of the rapidly approaching waters, one of the workers made a mobile phone call to the emergency services. It was too late. Some cocklers managed to struggle to the distant shore, but the rapidity with which the incoming tide was filling the channels around the now isolated sandbanks trapped the remainder. As the tide covered the sands, at least 21 are known to have drowned.

What happened next?

In March 2006 the gangmasters were convicted of manslaughter and breaches of immigration law at Preston Crown Court, and were sent to prison. One was jailed for 14 years and ordered to be deported at the end of his sentence.

Lessons

It is unusual for a disaster to be caused by someone's intentional criminal behaviour, but in this case the law was deliberately being evaded. The tragic accident revealed shockingly bad employment practices, exposing the careless exploitation of poorly paid illegal immigrant workers who were desperate for work. The public was appalled that it had resulted in so many deaths.

Demands for something to be done to prevent a repetition of such a tragedy led to the passing of the Gangmasters Licensing Act 2004 and the formation of the Gangmasters Licensing Authority to regulate those who supply labour or provide services in agriculture, forestry, horticulture, shellfish gathering, and food processing and packaging. Trade unions continue to press for its remit to be expanded to include the construction industry.

Sources

Milford Haven

Health and Safety Executive. The explosion and fires at the Texaco refinery, Milford Haven, 24th July 1994. www.hse.gov.uk/comah/sragtech/casetexaco94.htm

Windsor Castle

1992: Blaze rages in Windsor Castle. BBC News Online: On this day, 20 November. http://news.bbc.co.uk/onthisday/hi/dates/stories/november/20/newsid_2551000/2551107.stm

Camelford

Camelford poisoning hearings begin. BBC News Online, 3 April 2002. http://news.bbc.co.uk/1/hi/england/1908534.stm
Committee on Toxicity. COT Lowermoor Sub-group. http://cot.food.gov.uk/cotwg/lowermoorsub

Toulouse

French Environment Ministry. *Usine de la société Grande Paroisse à Toulouse: Accident du 21 septembre 2001* (in French). Paris: Ministère de l'Amenagement du Territoire et de l'Environnement, 2001. www.ecologie.gouv.fr/IMG/pdf/1024-explosion-toulouse-rapport.pdf

Morecambe Bay

BBC News Online. Tide kills 18 cockle pickers, 6 February 2004. http://news.bbc.co.uk/1/hi/england/lancashire/3464203.stm
BBC News Online. Cockle pickers died of drowning, 22 June 2004. http://news.bbc.co.uk/1/hi/england/lancashire/3827623.stm

Chapter 23: Safety culture under strain

A robust safety culture will always serve a company well, and if well established it should normally be resilient in the face of sudden stresses, but even so, it cannot provide a guarantee of immunity to every setback. Determined leadership and persistence will be necessary to repair any damage suffered, which may sometimes require more than simply rebuilding a plant.

There is much for everyone to learn from the difficulties experienced by an iconic British company with a hard-earned reputation for safety about the challenges of managing change and establishing a new safety culture.

The explosion at Texas City, USA, 2005

The BP Group acquired the Texas City refinery, together with its local workforce, from an American petrochemical company in 2001. It was the company's largest and most complex facility. It soon became clear from 'climate surveys' that the workforce was mistrustful of management. Confident, however, that it could embed its own high standards and culture at the plant, BP set about clarifying the standards of competence and the safety culture that it had inherited. Much was achieved between 2001 and 2004 to address safety issues, but all this was not enough to prevent a truly disastrous occurrence.

What happened and why?

Within the refinery, an isomerisation unit converted raffinate, a low octane blending feed, into higher octane components for regular unleaded petrol. This unit included a splitter, which fractionated raffinate into light and heavy liquids. The splitter itself consisted of a surge drum, a reboiler and a fractionating column (or tower) about 50 metres high.

On 23 March 2005 a massive explosion occurred at the raffinate unit, followed by fires.

At first sight the cause might seem to have been a simple human mistake, followed by others that made matters worse. During start-up, the operators had wrongly allowed flammable liquid to be pumped into the splitter tower for over three hours, overfilling it 20 times higher than the level specified in the start-up instructions. The operators compounded their initial error by then failing to take effective action to deal with the overfilling. The tower's contents overheated, over-pressurised the plant and blew the relief valves, venting towards temporary offices located only 150 feet away. The operators then failed to sound evacuation alarms.

The escaping flammable gas cloud inevitably found a source of ignition, wrecking the surrounding plant. The human consequences of the explosion were made worse by the proximity of temporary office accommodation for workers engaged on a turnaround of another section of plant. These offices were in trailers sited close by the raffinate unit and they were destroyed by the blast and fires. Fifteen workers were killed, some of them caught in the trailers, and many more were injured.

This awful catastrophe had resulted from a catalogue of errors at first sight stemming from the operational failures described above. However, these were not the root causes of the disaster, as internal and independent investigations were to show.

The aftermath of the explosion at BP Texas City, 23 March 2005. *US Chemical Safety and Hazard Investigation Board*

What happened next?

The group's chief executive officer, Lord Browne, flew to Texas City immediately after the explosion, where he emphasised that BP was responsible for what happens inside the boundaries of its sites and that this incident was no exception. He promised support to the victims of this tragedy and their families and that BP would apply its full resources to determine the cause of the explosion and fire, making it clear that the company would take any action necessary to prevent a recurrence. He guaranteed full co-operation with the investigating agencies and to share lessons learned with others.

Several investigations now ran concurrently. OSHA, the federal agency, was to allege over 300 separate violations of regulations, resulting in the company agreeing to pay a fine of more than $20 million and take certain steps, such as appointing experts to the Texas City site, without having to admit to the specific allegations.

A separate independent Chemical Safety and Hazard Investigation Board (CSB) had been set up some years earlier in the USA to conduct investigations of major incidents in the chemical process industries. The CSB's investigation led to industry-wide recommendations on the location of temporary buildings within refineries and to a recommendation that BP should establish an independent panel of experts to assess the adequacy of the safety management of all five of its US refineries.

The company agreed to this. The panel was led by the former US Secretary of State James A Baker and resulted in the 'Baker Report', which contained numerous further recommendations. While co-operating fully with these inquiries, BP rightly decided it should conduct its own investigation. While this enabled it to resist some of the findings of other investigations with which it did not agree, the company's unflinching approach to self-scrutiny is creditable and reveals how a willingness to be open and learn lessons from the bitter ashes of a disaster can strengthen corporate culture and rebuild reputation and trust.

The company had been shaken to the core by this disaster. It had believed profoundly in the strength of its safety culture, the company's standards which had developed over many years, its safety management systems, and the evidence of its audit programmes and statistics, showing how in its US operations the company had reduced its OSHA recordable injury rate by almost 70 per cent and its fatality rate by 75 per cent over the previous five years. What could possibly have gone wrong?

A team of BP operations, refining and safety experts and salaried and union employees at the Texas City refinery was formed and given terms of reference to determine the cause of the explosion and make recommendations for preventing similar incidents in the future. John Mogford, a senior vice-president from BP's offshore operations, led the investigation and brought his offshore experience to bear on what the team uncovered. He reported the findings to a conference of the Center for Chemical Process Safety in Orlando (the full text of his interesting address can be found at www.aiche.org/ccps or at www.bp.com), identifying five main underlying causes:

- Firstly, over the years the working environment had eroded to one characterized by resistance to change and lack of trust, motivation and purpose. Expectations around supervisory and management behaviour were unclear. Rules were not followed consistently. Individuals felt disempowered from suggesting or initiating improvements.
- Secondly, process safety, operations performance and systematic risk reduction priorities had not been set nor consistently reinforced by management. Safety lessons from other parts of BP were not acted on.
- Thirdly, many changes in a complex organization – both of structure and personnel – led to a lack of clear accountabilities and poor communication. The result was workforce confusion over roles, responsibilities and priorities.
- The fourth cause focused on poor hazard awareness and understanding of process safety on the site – resulting in people accepting higher levels of risk.
- And finally, poor performance management and vertical communication in the refinery meant there was no adequate early warning system of problems and no independent means of understanding the deteriorating standards in the plant through thorough audit of the organization.

Lessons
BP's own investigation made 81 recommendations to itself, too many to detail here. The main lessons learned were summarised by John Mogford as follows:

- The need to ensure plant leadership teams have the time to focus on day-to-day operations and aren't distracted by too many competing demands. Managers need to know what's happening in their control rooms and on the plant.
- The need to capture the right metrics that indicate process safety trends; do not get seduced by personal accident measures, they have their place but do not warn of incidents such as this one.
- Procedures are ineffective if they are not up-to-date and routinely followed
- The importance of two-way communication. If people believe leaders aren't listening or don't appear to be taking team members' concerns

seriously, then soon they stop raising them. We must keep our promises to each other. It's the first step in rebuilding trust and the only way to earn the respect and obtain the commitment of the workforce. This is about staying in touch, being aware, being responsible and listening.

- The importance of investigating process incidents and loss of containment incidents the same way serious injuries are investigated. Document all incidents thoroughly. Share what you learn.
- The value of having an effective feedback loop to capture and incorporate into operating procedures and training programs lessons learned from earlier incidents and process upsets.
- And lastly, keep non-essential personnel out of process areas. Take a hard look at any potential blast impact zones. And if you must have temporary structures near process areas make sure they are blast resistant. The safest way to protect your people is to move them outside of blast zones.

All this was absolutely right.

Sources

Baker J A *et al. The report of the BP U.S. refineries independent safety review panel* (the Baker Report), 2007. www.bp.com/bakerpanelreport
BP website, www.bp.com
Center for Chemical Process Safety, www.aiche.org/ccps
Health and Safety Executive. *BP Texas City incident.* London: HSE, 2007. www.hse.gov.uk/leadership/bakerreport.pdf
US Chemical Safety and Hazard Investigation Board, www.csb.gov

Chapter 24: Structural collapses

The Tay Bridge disaster, Scotland, 1879

> Beautiful Railway Bridge of the Silv'ry Tay!
> Alas! I am very sorry to say
> That ninety lives have been taken away
> On the last Sabbath day of 1879,
> Which will be remember'd for a very long time
> 'Twas about seven o'clock at night,
> And the wind it blew with all its might...
> And the Demon of the air seem'd to say –
> "I'll blow down the Bridge of Tay."

William McGonagall's famously bad poem about the worst bridge collapse of Victorian times is not strictly accurate as to the facts.

What happened?
During a gale on the night of 28 December 1879, the central spans of the new Tay Bridge collapsed into the Firth of Tay, Scotland, at 7.15 pm while a passenger train with six carriages was crossing towards Dundee. Seventy-five people died in this shocking disaster.

The remains of the Tay Bridge after its collapse on 28 December 1879.

The Tay Bridge had been opened only a year and a half earlier. It was a modern-day wonder. Designed and built by Thomas Bouch, a distinguished structural engineer of the period who had built other bridges to a similar design, the bridge was almost two miles long, the longest in the world at the time.

The bridge consisted of 85 lattice ironwork spans in all, supported on cast iron columns. In the centre were 13 'navigation spans' designed to allow tall ships to pass under the bridge. Unlike the rest of the bridge, where the single track railway was carried above the spans, these central navigation spans formed a 27-foot high tunnel of lattice ironwork through which the train would pass. It was these that failed and collapsed into the waters of the Firth some 88 feet below, taking the train and its passengers with them that stormy night.

Why?
Faulty design and construction were blamed for weaknesses in the structure which was unable that night to withstand the pressure of the wind – said to have been gusting up to Force 10 or 11.

What happened next?
Bouch had been knighted after completing the Tay Bridge and was already working on a design for the Forth Bridge, yet to be built. His reputation was at its height until this tragedy occurred.

An inquiry was held, in which many experts gave their opinion as to the likely cause of the structural failure, considering issues such as cost cutting, a possible derailment, metal fatigue, weather and design. The cause remains controversial but the consensus reached was that the bridge was simply not strong enough to withstand the pressure of high winds and that it should have been designed and built to meet the worst weather conditions that could have been expected on the Firth of Tay. Rightly or wrongly, Sir Thomas Bouch, whose son-in-law had been killed in the accident, was held chiefly responsible. The design and construction of the Forth Bridge was handed over to rival engineers and within a year Sir Thomas had died.

Lessons
It is fair to say that lessons were learnt. A second Tay Bridge was built soon afterwards and opened in 1887. It still stands today alongside the visible remains of the first, a stark reminder of the disaster.

In spite of the shock that had been dealt to the engineering profession by the Tay Bridge disaster, the building of a railway bridge across the Firth of

Forth also went ahead, but not to Sir Thomas Bouch's design. Some would say that it is hugely over-engineered, and that might well have been to ensure that it could never collapse.

Much painted and repaired, the iconic Forth Bridge still stands proudly today, a monument to Victorian engineering. It was also to become a wonder of the world and its completion was certainly a triumph over adversity. What is less well known is the heavy toll of fatal accidents that was the price that had to be paid for its construction: some 80 labourers' lives were lost, one by one, in the several years that it took to complete.

But this was never regarded as disastrous.

The Tacoma Narrows Bridge collapse, Washington State, 1940

Bridge building continued to evolve. Suspension bridges soon began to replace the heavily engineered ironwork of the 19th century and box girder bridges made their first appearance soon afterwards. Today these are the most commonly used designs for major bridges being built throughout the world. But disaster has sometimes accompanied their development.

The collapse of the Tacoma Narrows Bridge, 7 November 1940.
Smithsonian Institution

What happened and why?
The Tacoma Narrows Bridge in Washington State, USA, was a suspension road bridge built across Puget Sound. It was about half a mile long. On 7 November 1940 high winds caused the bridge to begin to sway. It gathered momentum and finally collapsed. Fortunately, by then no one was left on the bridge, although one motorist had a lucky escape and lost his car and his dog. As in the Tay Bridge disaster, faulty design was suspected.

Lessons
Suspension bridges had already been in use for more than 100 years when the Tacoma Narrows Bridge collapsed but this catastrophic failure sent structural engineers back to their drawing boards. The advancing sciences of aerodynamics and computer modelling soon came to their aid.

The Millennium Bridge, London, 2000
Even so, mistakes can still be made. The opening of the pedestrian footbridge built across the River Thames between St Paul's Cathedral and Bankside to celebrate the new millennium was fortunately only a PR disaster when it began to wobble under the impetus of hundreds of feet marching across it. There were no injuries and little risk of total collapse but embarrassing delays occurred while expensive modifications were made, and it is still remembered as the 'wobbly bridge'.

Bridges are not, of course, the only structures susceptible to sudden collapse if there are flaws in design or construction.

Ronan Point, London, 1968
During the 1960s, tower blocks of flats were being erected in cities everywhere to relieve housing shortages. But a gas explosion was soon to lead to radical rethinking of their design and construction.

What happened?
Ronan Point was a 22-storey tower (about 200 feet high) recently built in Newham, east London. On 16 May 1968 at six o'clock in the morning, an explosion blew out the walls of the living room in a flat on the 18th floor, leaving the four floors above unsupported. These collapsed onto the lounge of the flat on the floor below which could not withstand the extra load and gave way in turn. Gathering ever more weight as it fell, the heavy concrete wreckage cascaded from floor to floor, taking out one corner lounge after another in a vertical domino effect, until the corner units of all 22 floors in the block had been completely destroyed.
Four residents were killed and 17 injured, a remarkably small number considering that the block was home to 260 people. Fortunately, at that

The 'domino effect' of the gas explosion at Ronan Point, 16 May 1968
Popperfoto/ Getty Images

time of the morning most were still in their bedrooms as their lounges were sliced away.

Why?
There was a gas supply to the block and a leak caused the explosion that triggered the collapse.

However, the collapse might have been avoided had the tower block been designed and constructed differently. The block had been built like many others at that time using large prefabricated concrete panels which were fastened together on site to form load-bearing walls, floors and roofs (known as the Larsen-Nielsen system of construction).

Originally, this Danish system had been limited in Denmark to use in buildings no more than six storeys high.

What happened next?
An inquiry into what had caused the disaster was held under Hugh
Griffiths QC, who reported in November 1968. He and his expert
colleagues found that the behaviour of the building was inherent in its
design and was not due to faulty workmanship. His report stated that
progressive collapse after such an accident can be avoided by the
introduction of sufficient steel reinforcement to provide effective ties at the
joints between the structural components, and by so arranging the
components that loads can be carried in alternative ways if a failure occurs.

The report also recommended that existing blocks in large panel
construction over six storeys in height should be structurally appraised
and where necessary strengthened. It recommended that the gas supply
should be cut off in any blocks judged susceptible to progressive collapse
until they had been strengthened. Provided that the danger of progressive
collapse was removed, it found no reason to prohibit the use of gas in
high buildings, and no reason why forms of construction using large pre-
cast concrete panels should be discontinued. Instead it recommended that
the Building Regulations should be revised to deal with those risks.

Ronan Point was repaired by tying a freestanding, self-supporting corner
unit into the original structure. The tower was finally demolished in
1986.

Lessons
The inherent weakness of the joints connecting the panels meant that a
flank wall could easily be blown out. The remaining structure would not
be strong enough to support the weight of floors above and would be
prone to the progressive collapse that occurred at Ronan Point.

Port Ramsgate, England, 1994
In 1994 an unusual structural collapse occurred, causing multiple fatalities
at the port of Ramsgate in Kent.

What happened?
Port Ramsgate operated a cross-Channel ferry service to Belgium. During
the night of 14 September, passengers were boarding a cross-Channel ferry
by way of a recently installed elevated walkway from the terminal
building to the ship when it suddenly gave way and fell 30 feet to the
ground. Six passengers were killed and seven were seriously hurt.

Why?
Just one steel pin held the walkway in place between the ferries and the
terminal building. Four sliding feet supporting the walkway at its far end

The collapsed
walkway at Port
Ramsgate,
14 September 1994.
David Eves

were intended to allow for movement of the vessel. A weld broke and this
was sufficient to cause the entire structure to fall.

What happened next?
The HSE investigated and found evidence that the use of inferior steel,
inaccurate design and substandard welding aligning the feet to the
walkway had caused the accident. The walkway had been too rigid and
the feet too small to withstand its weight and the weight of passengers
using it. The HSE prosecuted four companies in connection with the
accident, arguing successfully that inaccurate design calculations, inferior
steel and bad workmanship had meant the walkway was an accident
waiting to happen.

The court imposed record fines totalling more than £1 million on the four
defendants. Lloyds Register of Shipping, which had given the walkway the
all-clear before it was taken into use, pleaded guilty to the charge that it
failed to ensure the safety of passengers by properly checking the equipment.
Port Ramsgate, the operator, defended the charges against it but was also
found guilty and fined. Two Swedish companies, Fartygsentreprenader AB
and Fartygskonstruktioner AB, which had designed and installed the
structure, pleaded not guilty. They failed to attend the hearing at the Old
Bailey but were convicted in their absence. Declaring themselves bankrupt,
the Swedish companies never paid their fines.

Lessons
Fixed metal fabricated structures subjected to movement have to be specifically designed to take account of stresses and loadings. While the trigger for the structural failure in this case was simply the breakage of one poorly welded component, the design of the walkway was inherently unsafe. Using components of inferior quality and welding them together poorly added insult to injury.

Sources

Tay Bridge
Tay Bridge Disaster: Report of the Court of Inquiry, and report of Mr Rothery, upon the circumstances attending the fall of a portion of the Tay Bridge on the 28th December 1879. London: HMSO, 1880. www.railwaysarchive.co.uk/documents/ BoT_TayInquiry1880.pdf
Tom Martin's Tay Bridge disaster webpages, http://taybridgedisaster.co.uk/index/index

Tacoma Narrows Bridge
University of Washington Digital Collection. Tacoma Narrows Bridge Collection. http://content.lib.washington.edu/farquharsonweb/index.html
Video footage of the collapse, www.youtube.com/watch?v=3mclp9QmCGs.

Millennium Bridge
Dallard P *et al.* The London Millennium Footbridge. *Structural Engineer*, 20 November 2001; 79 (22): 17–35. www.arup.com/MillenniumBridge/indepth/pdf/IStructE.pdf

Ronan Point
1968: Three die as tower block collapses. BBC News Online: On this day, 16 May. http://news.bbc.co.uk/onthisday/hi/dates/stories/may/16/newsid_2514000/2514277.stm
Lal Amy. Events in local history – Ronan Point. www.lalamy.demon.co.uk/ronanpnt.htm

Port Ramsgate
Health and Safety Executive. *Walkway collapse at Port Ramsgate.* Sudbury: HSE Books, 2000

Chapter 25: Floods

Floods might seem simply another natural disaster, but we have sometimes contributed to a flooding catastrophe when we have failed in an attempt to harness water for our own purposes or to take adequate steps to protect ourselves against sudden inundations.

Most visitors to Fréjus in the south of France will be happily unaware that in 1959 the recently completed Malpasset dam on the river Reyran burst only a few kilometres away, sending a mighty wall of water rushing down the valley and through the ancient Roman town to the sea. More than 400 people were killed. The failure of the concrete dam was partially due to its arch design being combined with unstable local geological features that had not been adequately surveyed. Heavy rainfall overfilled the reservoir until the wall suddenly gave way under the enormous pressure.

It is even less likely that visitors to Sheffield in northern England will have heard of a somewhat similar event that occurred nearly 150 years ago, involving a reservoir retained by a large earth dam.

The Dale Dike dam disaster, Sheffield, England, 1864

Dam failures may seem unusual in this country, but on 11 March 1864 the Dale Dike dam holding a newly constructed drinking water reservoir at Bradfield, near Sheffield, collapsed after the reservoir had been filled for the first time, releasing an estimated 3 million tonnes of water. This enormous volume surged down the valley of the River Loxley until, meeting the River Don, it rushed into Sheffield, destroying 800 houses and 15 bridges in its path and inundating the city centre, killing 270 people. The disaster came to be known as 'the Great Sheffield Flood'.

An inquiry concluded, unsurprisingly, that the construction of the dam was faulty. The dam had taken three years to build. It was a massive earthwork 500 feet wide at the base, 100 feet high and 12 feet wide at the top. A small leak in the dam wall had grown rapidly until the whole structure failed catastrophically.

In June 2007 the River Don was overtopped by heavy rainfall and Sheffield was flooded again. Further down the Don valley, 700 residents had to be evacuated from the village of Catcliffe after cracks appeared in the brimful Ulley Reservoir dam. If the dam had failed the reservoir would have seriously threatened the town of Rotherham lying further downstream; fortunately, engineers managed to relieve the pressure by pumping millions of gallons from the reservoir, and the dam held.

Lynmouth, Devon, England, 1952

The residents of Lynmouth, north Devon, had not been so fortunate.
Lynmouth lay at the foot of a steep valley in which the East and West Lyn
rivers converged, draining the wide expanses of Exmoor a few miles
above. Its twin village of Lynton was at the top of the hill.

That August it had rained very heavily for the first two weeks and the
moors above the villages were saturated, unable to absorb any more water.
On the night of 15 August 1952 another torrential downpour over Exmoor
burst the banks of the many streams that fed the normally placid East and
West Lyn rivers. By the time they reached their confluence at Lynton they
had become raging torrents, sweeping great boulders and trees before them.
As these jammed against obstructions, temporary dams were formed that
burst without warning, releasing a prodigious weight of water.

Lying at the foot of the steep valley, with its houses nestling between the
steep hillsides and the river, Lynmouth was doomed that night. Thirty-four
people lost their lives, washed away with their homes and drowned.

North Sea storm surge, England, The Netherlands and Belgium, 1953

Worse still was the disastrous flooding of the Netherlands and the East Anglian and Thames Estuary coasts in England in 1953. As a young schoolboy, in those days I was travelling by train from Gravesend to Rochester across the north Kent marshes, an evocative landscape immortalised by Charles Dickens in *Great Expectations*. The floods had caused the Southern Electric line to be suspended but the old steam locomotives were still able to make their way along the raised track, just a foot or two above a new seascape that for several days in February stretched eerily across the estuary, as far as the eye could see. Years were to pass before I learnt that 307 people had lost their lives along the English coast as their homes were inundated by the tidal surge.

What happened and why?

On the night of Saturday 31 January 1953, very high winds across the North Sea and a spring tide combined to create a tidal surge well over 15 feet above normal, utterly overwhelming the sea defences in East Anglia and the Thames estuary and inundating vast tracts of low-lying land. During the storm, 230 lives were lost at sea that night. A further 30,000 people had to be evacuated from their homes and 24,000 properties were seriously damaged.

Across the sea, the consequences were even more horrific. By the following day, 1 February, 30,000 animals had been drowned and 1,835 people had lost their lives in the Netherlands. In Belgium, 28 perished. Had it not been for the heroic efforts of the emergency services, it could

Red Cross staff deliver supplies to victims of the Lynmouth flood, 1952.
British Red Cross Museum and Archives

Floods in Zuid
Beveland, The
Netherlands, in 1953.
US Army

have been far worse. In the Netherlands 70,000 people were safely evacuated from their homes.

There had been no disaster warnings as local radio stations did not broadcast at night. Telephone networks were soon disrupted and as the disaster struck on a Saturday night, offices were largely unmanned. Three million people were at risk if one of the Dutch dykes had failed: when it began to collapse on 1 February the local mayor insisted that a ship be sailed into the breach to plug the gap. Incredibly, it worked.

Lessons
As is so often the case, the stable door was shut too late to prevent the disaster. The Dutch government set up a commission to study the causes and effects of the floods. This led to the 'Delta Works', an ambitious but ultimately highly successful flood defence system completed in 1998.
In the UK, the event triggered investment in coastal defences in the hope of preventing a repetition of the tragedy. Twenty years still had to pass before it was decided to build a barrage to protect London against another storm surge. In 1928, 14 people had died in London when the Thames flooded.

The Thames Barrier, the second largest of its kind in the world, was built between 1974 and 1982 at a cost of some £600 million, including £100 million for other river defences. It was finished in the nick of time. The Barrier had to be closed in earnest in 1983, before its official opening by the Queen in 1984. It has since closed over 100 times.

Scientists are warning that global warming is causing rising sea levels, but it is unclear whether this will be a slow gradual process, allowing a dignified, planned retreat from low-lying coastal areas, or whether further great storm surges are more likely.

In recent years, major improvements have been carried out to protect the London Underground system against flooding (the top risk for the Underground, even exceeding fire or attacks by terrorists). But who knows how many lives could be lost in London if the Barrier were to fail? Plans to build further defences in the Thames estuary are presently on hold.

Boscastle, Cornwall, England, 2004

Fifty-two years to the day after the Lynmouth flooding, the residents and tourists visiting Boscastle were fortunate to be saved when the three small rivers that converged on the picturesque fishing village were overfilled by a heavy downpour on Bodmin Moor, and raged through the village to the sea.

Flooding in Boscastle, Cornwall, 16 August 2004.
James Arthan-Searle, University of Portsmouth

After Lynmouth, it should have been obvious that Boscastle, sharing a similar topography, was an accident waiting to happen. The authorities had not prepared for this eventuality. Luckily, although many people were trapped in buildings no one was drowned, but the damage to property was extensive. Flood defences have since been improved and withstood the test of more heavy rain in the summer of 2009.

But as I write this, Cockermouth in Cumbria has been flooded after the heaviest rainfall for many years, and in Workington a policeman leading people to safety has been swept to his death from the Northside Bridge as it collapsed under the force of the swollen river, reminding us that disaster is never very far away.

Sources

Dale Dike

Armitage M. The Great Flood at Sheffield – 1864. http://mick-armitage.staff.shef.ac.uk/sheffield/flood.html
The story of the Sheffield Flood. www.rotherhamweb.co.uk/h/extracts/flood.htm

Lynmouth

1952: Flood devastates Devon village. BBC News Online: On this day, 16 August. http://news.bbc.co.uk/onthisday/hi/dates/stories/august/16/newsid_2960000/2960180.stm
Delderfield E R. *The Lynmouth flood disaster.* ERD Books, 1969

North Sea

BBC Weather. The 1953 East Coast floods. www.bbc.co.uk/weather/features/understanding/1953_flood.shtml
Pollard M. *North Sea surge: story of the East Coast floods of 1953.* London: Terence Dalton, 1982

Boscastle

BBC News Online. Boscastle gets rebuild go-ahead, 12 January 2005. http://news.bbc.co.uk/1/hi/england/cornwall/4167707.stm
Meteorological Office. Boscastle flood – 16 August 2004. www.metoffice.gov.uk/corporate/library/dws/Boscastle_Flood-16_August_2004.pdf

Chapter 26: Silent killers at work

The word 'disaster' is not usually associated with occupational health problems but in some cases it seems quite appropriate. Diseases caused by carcinogenic and toxic substances are silent and slow, unnoticed at first, harming or killing in ones or twos but taking their toll of scores of thousands over the decades.

Asbestos
Asbestos is a naturally occurring fibrous mineral found in certain parts of the world and it has been mined since Roman times. Its fire-resisting properties were long understood, but it was only when industrial use increased massively towards the end of the 19th century that its cost to human health began to emerge.

Asbestos has saved many lives, for example in the form of fire protection insulation materials in ships and buildings, or asbestos cement products such as pipes bringing clean water to remote parts of the developing world. But it has also killed thousands who have inhaled asbestos fibres in the course of their work and it will kill many more. Exposure to the fibres may cause mesothelioma, a form of cancer that is always fatal, lung cancer, which is usually fatal, and asbestosis and diffuse pleural thickening, which may not be fatal but can be severely debilitating.

The Control of Asbestos Regulations 2006 are the latest step in the UK's attempts to control the risk after a century of faltering discovery that asbestos was one of the most hazardous materials in use. It is an unhappy story. For many years a lack of sufficient research, leading to limited understanding of the risks by the medical and scientific professions, a failure to communicate risks effectively, regulatory delays by governments until more evidence emerged, and employers' disregard of the risks to their workers in the absence of an enforceable legal standard, all contributed towards a heavy cost for its widespread use: the lives of countless workers and members of the public.

The HSE estimates that 4,000 people still die every year in the UK from the effects of exposure to this carcinogenic material, and even now a new generation of workers is still being put at risk by ignorance, incompetence or blatant disregard of the law.

What happened?
In 1893 Her Majesty's first female Inspectors of Factories had been appointed in Great Britain. Great credit should be given to Miss Deane,

This worker in the South African asbestos fields is surrounded by crocidolite asbestos.
Tim Carter

Miss Paterson and Dame Adelaide Anderson for being among the first to draw attention to the health risks from inhaling asbestos fibres, leading to a new industrial disease, asbestosis, for which there was (and still is) no cure. In those days it was common for asbestos workers to be surrounded by a fog of dust caused by the millions of microscopic fibres given off during processing. In the absence of any effective protective equipment, some of this dust was bound to be inhaled or ingested.

Why?
Even during the first half of the 20th century, medical and scientific understanding of the hazards of asbestos still lagged way behind the increasing use of this remarkable fire-resistant natural material. For many years the dust was regarded as more of a nuisance than a hazard. Workers would return home with their clothing contaminated, and expose their families to what the press have since branded 'the deadly dust'. As workers' lung function diminished, symptoms such as shortness of breath would gradually emerge. By then there was no way back to health.

Asbestos was now being used in all sorts of applications: lagging boilers, protecting buildings and warships from fire, in textiles and building materials, vehicle brakes and clutches.

What happened next?
Yet it was not until 1931 that the first regulations to control the use of asbestos at work were made. These only covered certain specified

processes, such as the manufacture of asbestos mattresses used for insulation. Other potentially hazardous processes, such as the spraying of asbestos onto steelwork for fire protection, or the stripping of asbestos during ship-breaking or demolition activities, were not covered by the law and would not be controlled for many years to come.

The Second World War intervened and brought research into the health effects of asbestos to a halt. More health problems began to emerge after the war, when many ships were being broken up and old power stations demolished. Even so, it was not until the 1960s that it began to dawn that the material was a carcinogen. There can be a very long period of latency before an individual begins to display symptoms of asbestos-related disease.

First, a link between asbestos and lung cancer began to emerge. It was then noticed that cases of mesothelioma, a cancer of the lining of the body's internal organs, seemed to be linked to exposure to the fibres of blue asbestos (crocidolite). Cancer, a dreaded disease, was now laid at the door of 'the deadly dust' and there had to be a political reaction. The government formed an Asbestos Advisory Committee to consider how best to control the risks and it soon decided that brown and blue asbestos were the chief culprits. White asbestos – commonly used in building materials – was thought at the time to be less hazardous.

Cigarette smoking was very common among the workforce at that time. Exposure to tobacco smoke was an added complication for doctors and scientists and some suspected that for many individuals it worsened the effects of their asbestos exposure.

However, progress was still painfully slow. Two new sets of regulations were eventually made in 1985, banning the importation, supply and use of blue and brown asbestos in workplaces. In 1984 another set of regulations had introduced licensing of operators specialising in asbestos removal. Only licensed, properly equipped operators were allowed to do this hazardous work.

Use of white asbestos, mistakenly thought to be less problematic, was finally banned by the UK in 1999. In the meantime the European Commission was developing its own policies and an EU Directive eventually laid down the standards to be applied across the European Union. This necessitated the UK revising its own standards.

Finally, after much further consideration and debate, the Control of Asbestos Regulations 2006 have brought together the three earlier sets of regulations covering prohibition, control of asbestos at work and licensing. The new regulations prohibit the importation, supply and use of all forms of asbestos.

Lessons
The long latency period of asbestos-related diseases means that deaths caused by asbestos exposure will continue to occur for many years to come. There are still many thousands of tonnes of asbestos remaining in buildings and equipment yet to be decommissioned. It is sensible to leave well-protected asbestos material where it is in good condition and unlikely to suffer damage. But when any work with asbestos or which may disturb asbestos is being carried out, for example building refurbishment or demolition work, it is vital that employers keep worker exposure below the control limit for airborne asbestos dust.

It remains to be seen whether the latest laws make a real difference. The effectiveness of the regulations will need to be kept under review as new generations of plasterers, electricians, plumbers and carpenters will continue to encounter the material in buildings. Their employers must protect them by complying with the high standards now enshrined in health and safety law, which the regulatory authorities must strictly enforce.

After I joined HM Factory Inspectorate in 1964, during my training I was taken to a large factory in east London processing asbestos to observe compliance with the 1931 Asbestos Regulations – at that time still the only law applicable apart from Section 63 of the Factories Act 1961, which covered dust in general. I soon learnt that my experienced colleagues regarded the 1931 Regulations and Section 63 as feeble and unenforceable. In fact, so far as I know there was only ever one prosecution under the 1931 Regulations – of the Central Asbestos Company, by an inspector, John Fallaize.

Tribute must be paid here to the late Dr Robert Murray of the TUC for his tireless work over many years to raise awareness of the risks from asbestos, and to Bryan Harvey, former Chief Inspector of Factories and first Deputy Director of the HSE, who campaigned long and hard for legally enforceable controls.

In the meantime it remains appalling that miners of asbestos in some countries continue to be exposed to clouds of the 'deadly dust'. This must be the next challenge for the international community to address.

Lead poisoning
Appointed factory doctors, Medical Inspectors of Factories and later the staff of the Employment Medical Advisory Service have all played a significant role over the decades in identifying the causes and finding

solutions to preventing the numerous diseases caused by exposure to toxic substances in the workplace.

Lead was commonly used in many industrial processes throughout the 19th century and realisation that it caused serious health problems was slow in coming. The first controls over exposure to lead at work originated from the use of glazes containing lead in the pottery industry and the introduction of lead-free glazes, a classic case of being able to substitute a less dangerous substance.

Where substitution was impossible, the imperfect understanding of how to control toxic dust or fumes by engineering measures such as ventilation, personal protective equipment and good hygiene meant that workers' health would continue to be in jeopardy until some crisis occurred that demanded political action. A hundred years ago, prohibition seemed the only available means of controlling risks to health from very toxic substances. An example was the banning of the use of white or yellow phosphorus in the manufacture of 'Lucifer' matches following public outrage at the ravages of 'phossy jaw', which disfigured the 'match girls' of the East End of London.

Even in the late 20th century, by which time the prevention of lead poisoning was far better understood, the problems continued. By the early 1970s things had begun to come to a head.

What happened?
Doctors identified several lead poisoning cases among schoolchildren in the East End and these were traced to exposure to dust escaping from Associated Lead's factory on the Isle of Dogs. While no children would die from this exposure, there was concern about longer-term damage to their health, and the press had a field day with the story.

The significance of all this was borne in on me when, during a spell working in headquarters as a junior inspector, I was asked by Bryan Harvey, then HM Chief Inspector of Factories, to review the Inspectorate's interventions at a smelting operation at Avonmouth, near Bristol.

Factory doctors had identified a worrying number of cases of lead absorption among the workforce at RTZ's Imperial Smelting Works and, like the cases on the Isle of Dogs, these had caught the attention of the media. As public concern began mounting, ministers became alarmed. The 'state of the art' plant at Avonmouth had been opened by the Queen and had been hailed as part of Prime Minister Harold Wilson's 'white hot technological revolution', pointing the way ahead for manufacturing in Britain.

Why?

While the press went about lambasting the company, the subtext of the story was: "Why had the Factory Inspectorate allowed this situation to develop?" This was to become a regular theme in the following decades. I recall taking a note of a meeting between Bryan Harvey and Sir Val Duncan, then the chairman of RTZ, at which the Chief Inspector warned him that unless conditions at the plant were brought under control he would be "forced to become more abrasive". I stored this useful phrase away for future reference but the truth was, at the time, that the Inspectorate's powers under the Factories Act to remedy matters were very limited.

However, bowing before the fierce gales of unwelcome attention, the company decided to close the plant for a few months in 1972 while essential modifications were made. When it reopened, careful monitoring of environmental air and the workforce showed that the problem had been brought under control.

What happened next?

At its peak, the number of notifiable lead poisonings at Avonmouth in a single year was less than a dozen cases, but incidents of lead absorption, the precursor of poisoning identified by sampling of lead in blood, had risen to around 40. The Inspectorate produced a report of their investigation for the minister in 1972, which prompted the government to establish a special committee of inquiry.

Lessons

The inquiry was led by Professor Bryan Windeyer, a member of the Robens Committee, which had been meeting since 1970 to consider how to improve the state of health and safety generally in Great Britain.

Windeyer found a number of causes of the lead exposures. Frequent machinery breakdowns had been occurring on the plant, and lead dust was escaping uncontrolled into the workers' breathing zones. Local management problems and the absence of an effective policy for the control of the lead hazard to health had simply compounded the effects of these difficulties. Windeyer recommended that in addition to improving the technical measures that were obviously needed to control and monitor the amounts of lead in the air at the plant, senior management had to recognise its responsibilities and develop a policy to protect the health of workers, who should be educated in risks to their health.

These were familiar themes. Windeyer's findings were to influence the greater emphasis that was to be placed on occupational health when the

Robens Committee reported its recommendations on the future regulation of health and safety in Great Britain that summer.

Carcinogens

While the list of chemicals that can do harm to humans is practically endless, we need to be able to work with them safely to gain the benefits they also bring. Like asbestos, the period of latency between exposure to a carcinogen and first showing symptoms can be very long and, by the time a diagnosis has been made, it is often too late to effect a cure. But research can help a looming problem from becoming a major disaster.

To take an example, in the British rubber manufacturing industry there had been a history of an increased risk of bladder cancers among workers. Studies pinned this down to exposure to a particular contaminant, beta-naphthylamine, which until 1949 had been present in the antioxidant 'Nonox S' used during the mixture of rubber compounds. The use of this substance was immediately stopped voluntarily. However, vigilance was maintained through continuing studies for the workforce. Reassuringly, it was eventually found that the incidence of bladder cancers was no longer excessive. But it was also noticed that between 1949 and 1976 there appeared to be an excessive incidence of lung and stomach cancers among rubber workers, possibly associated with exposure to rubber dust and fumes. Considerable efforts were made in the industry to control emissions during rubber processing, aiming at achieving half the workplace exposure limit agreed in consultation between the regulator and the industry.

A further study of workers exposed between 1982 and 1991 indicated that deaths and the incidence of lung and stomach cancer among rubber workers were not above the levels that would normally be seen in the general population.

Lessons

The rubber industry is an example of how a determined industry, alert to warning signs and ready to fund research, can successfully head off trouble by substituting safer chemicals, and taking the relatively simple measures required to control dust and fumes to as low a level as reasonably practicable, as required by law.

The close co-operation that has existed between the representatives of employers and trade unions on the Rubber Industry Advisory Committee has undoubtedly helped by creating an environment of mutual trust within which concerns can be openly discussed and solutions found.

Sources

Asbestos
Control of Asbestos Regulations 2006
Health and Safety Executive. Asbestos health and safety. www.hse.gov.uk/asbestos
Wagner J C, Sleggs C A and Marchand P. Diffuse pleural mesothelioma and asbestos
exposure in the north western Cape Province (with commentary by T Carter). *Policy and
Practice in Health and Safety* 2005; 3 (2) supplementary issue: 13–32

Lead poisoning
Control of Lead at Work Regulations 2002
Health and Safety Executive. Working safely with lead. www.hse.gov.uk/lead/index.htm

Carcinogens
Scorecard – the pollution information site. Carcinogens. www.scorecard.org/health-effects/
chemicals.tcl?short_hazard_name=cancer&all_p=t
Wikipedia. Carcinogen. http://en.wikipedia.org/wiki/Carcinogen

Chapter 27: Public health

In the 14th century, the Black Death swept into Europe from Central Asia, reaching Italy and France along the Mediterranean trade routes in 1347, and England via the port of Weymouth in 1348. Nothing much could be done about it. Medical science was still in its infancy and these occasional pestilences were regarded as Biblical acts of God. The Black Death (probably caused by bubonic plague, spread by rats) is believed to have killed one third of the European population before it petered out for a while, recurring mysteriously from time to time during the next 400 years.

Few who remember their history lessons can fail to be aware of the Great Plague suffered by London in 1665, followed a year later by the Great Fire. But it is easy to forget in 21st century Britain that only a century ago the population was still commonly exposed to outbreaks of some of the deadliest diseases known to man. Cholera, typhoid fever, diphtheria and smallpox were greatly feared, outbreaks were not at all uncommon, cures were as yet unknown and medical science was struggling to find solutions. Infant mortality was high, particularly among poorer families. It was thought safer to drink beer than water.

Cholera – the Broad Street pump, Soho, London, 1854
But thanks to pioneering Victorian doctors, scientists and engineers, things slowly began to improve. Never to be forgotten is the famous episode of the Broad Street pump. It heralded a much-needed breakthrough in controlling cholera by preventive measures and clean drinking water.

What happened?
Between 1831 and 1854 there had been four major outbreaks of cholera in the north east of England and in London. Over 10,000 people had died.

In 1854 cholera broke out in Soho, London, on 31 August. It is hard now for a visitor to believe that in those days people dwelt there cheek by jowl alongside live animals, their crumbling houses standing among cowsheds and slaughterhouses in deplorably overcrowded, insanitary conditions. Blocked drains, cesspools, rats and rubbish, and reliance on wells for drinking water, loaded the dice against public health.

Within three days 127 people had died in the vicinity of Broad Street and the wealthier local residents had begun shutting their shops and fleeing their homes. A week later the number of deaths had reached 500 and the numbers afflicted were increasing as the days went on.

Part of the map used
by John Snow to plot
cholera cases
contracted from the
Broad Street pump in
the 1854 epidemic.
John Snow

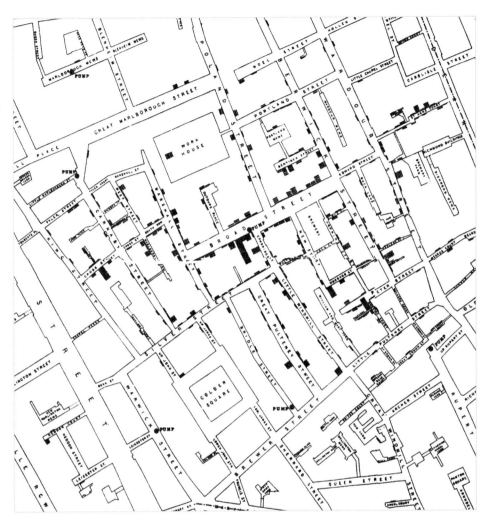

Why?

Dr John Snow, a local resident himself, lived in Frith Street, close by.
Already believing from his research that cholera was caught from water
contaminated with sewage, he stayed in Soho to do whatever he could.
What he did was to achieve a remarkable insight into the cause and
prevention of this deadly disease. He noticed that many victims drew their
water from the well in Broad Street, whereas there were very few victims
among those who used wells elsewhere. He took samples of water from
the Broad Street pump and found they contained "white, flocculent
particles", which he was convinced were the cause of the infections.

Snow reported his findings to a sceptical Board of Guardians of St James's
Parish, whose pump this was, and persuaded them to remove the pump
handle. Deprived of the water that was the source of the infection, the

remaining local citizens survived and the outbreak ended. By then 616 people had died.

There was other evidence to support Snow's deduction. Nearby was a brewery, whose workers drank only beer and never touched the water from the Broad Street well. None of these succumbed. Similarly, at a workhouse in nearby Poland Street, there were only five victims out of more than 500 inmates, most of whom had never drunk from the Broad Street supply.

What happened next?
Extraordinarily, Dr Snow's findings remained disputed. Even the local vicar persisted in believing that the outbreak had been an act of God. It was many years before the cesspits that presented such a risk to the wells were replaced by proper sewerage.

This kind of neglect of basic hygiene was not confined to London. There continued to be outbreaks of disease elsewhere and nowhere could be regarded as safe from them. One outbreak, possibly long forgotten, occurred in a Cornish market town, which is happily thronged these days by summer visitors.

Typhus – Wadebridge, Cornwall, England, 1897
In 1897 the Cornish market town of Wadebridge was struck by an outbreak of typhus. The deadly disease was not uncommon in Victorian England. This particular outbreak claimed 50 lives between 4 July and 26 September, when it died away in the strange manner of these events.

What happened and why?
Communications 100 years ago were poor. It was not until August that the outbreak was brought to the attention of the Local Government Board, and then it was reported as an instance of water-borne enteric fever.

The origin appeared to be a private water supply that had become contaminated by leaking drains and poorly constructed sewers serving buildings in the town's main street.

What happened next?
The Board demanded to know what the rural district council intended to do "to provide wholesome water and carry out other sanitary measures necessary for the place ... having in view the unsatisfactory nature of the water supply and other sanitary shortcomings of Wadebridge, which had again and again been commented on in the annual reports of the Medical Officer of Health."

Incredibly, little or nothing was done. It would be another 50 years before nationalisation of the private water companies allowed central intervention and the provision of proper sewers in the town.

Typhus and cholera outbreaks still occurred elsewhere. There was an outbreak of typhoid fever in Addington, Surrey in 1938, involving a private water supply.

Smallpox – Birmingham, England, 1978

It was believed by 1980 that another deadly disease, smallpox, had been totally eradicated, thanks to a successful worldwide programme of vaccination. However, a shocking case in Birmingham two years before had been a recent stark reminder of the virulence of this disease.

What happened and why?
Somehow, in September 1978, live smallpox virus was allowed to escape from laboratory facilities at Birmingham University, infecting a medical photographer who worked there. Initially misdiagnosed as simply suffering from a rash, she developed smallpox and died soon afterwards.

It is still not clear how the virus escaped. Dangerous pathogens kept for research are subject to the most rigorous controls and may only be handled in totally contained facilities by competent staff in fully protective kit.

What happened next?
This sad tale concluded with another death, the suicide of the head of the microbiological department. The university was prosecuted for breach of health and safety law and found not guilty.

The only remaining stocks of live smallpox virus are now kept – as far as anyone can be certain – in two closely guarded locations in Russia and the USA for the purposes of research.

Smallpox is rightly dreaded but there are many other micro-organisms capable of wreaking havoc among us. E. coli 0157 is one that has emerged only in the last 20 years, and it can now be found almost everywhere. Cattle often carry the virus, which does not harm them, and may excrete millions into the environment, where the virus may be spread by contact and ingested by humans. A number of outbreaks have occurred here and abroad, usually involving contaminated food.

The first case of food poisoning to be linked with the bug was recorded in 1986. Food poisoning is often associated with holidays abroad and 'Montezuma's revenge', but it is no laughing matter and can be lethal.

According to the Department of Health, an astonishing one in five people suffer an episode of food poisoning in the UK every year. Among the several bugs that cause it, *E. coli* 0157 is one that can have the worst effects, sometimes causing severe renal failure and death. Young children and the elderly are particularly vulnerable.

E. coli 0157 – Lanarkshire, Scotland, 1996
The UK's worst outbreak of *E. coli* infection – one of the world's worst in fact – originated from a butcher's shop of high repute in the small Scottish town of Wishaw, Lanarkshire.

What happened?
On Friday 22 November 1996 the Public Health Department of Lanarkshire Health Board became aware of several cases of *E. coli* among residents of Wishaw. Confirmed as *E. coli* 0157 by microbiological testing, the infection pointed towards an outbreak of food poisoning.

An outbreak control team was formed to investigate and control the outbreak and swiftly identified a common link between a number of the cases: consumption of food containing meat supplied by J Barr and Son, a local butcher. The butcher was running a substantial retail and wholesale business, employing about 40 staff in production and distribution of raw and cooked meats and bakery products to some 85 separate outlets in central Scotland, making the outbreak control team's task of tracing all the potential cases unusually difficult.

By the end of the outbreak, 496 cases linked to the Barr business had been identified, mainly among elderly people who are particularly vulnerable to the infection. About 100 of them had become infected after eating food at a birthday party in the church hall. Many were hospitalised and about 40 required kidney dialysis. Twenty-one died.

Why?
During the preparation of raw and cooked meats, it is essential to keep them separate, as cross-contamination can occur. Although there had been investment in modern equipment at the premises, the layout and design did not lend themselves to separation of raw and cooked meats, and some of the latter had been contaminated with the *E. coli* 0157 bacterium.

What happened next?
The business closed voluntarily on 27 November and the outbreak control team continued its work. The last case associated with the outbreak was identified on 15 December. Because deaths had occurred, under a procedure commonly adopted in Scottish law, a Fatal Accident Inquiry by

the Procurator Fiscal was set in train and led to the prosecution of the butcher, who was later found guilty by a jury of breaches of food safety law and fined £2,250.

Lessons
In the meantime a group of experts led by Professor Hugh Pennington of Aberdeen NHS Trust – known as 'the Pennington Group' – was asked to carry out an independent inquiry into the cause and control of the outbreak. The group examined a number of issues, including how and why fresh meat had become contaminated with *E. coli* 0157, the likely distribution in the food chain, measures that could be taken to minimise contamination and cross-contamination, how these measures could be enforced, and the steps that need to be taken once an outbreak has occurred to manage and control it. The group made a number of recommendations that were welcomed by the regulatory authorities.

Since 1995, all businesses that produce or handle food have been obliged to have in place a food safety management system, under which they must carry out hazard analysis and act to reduce the risks of food contamination. A Hazard Analysis and Critical Control Point plan (HACCP) has to be prepared and kept under review.

After the regulation of slaughterhouses and abattoirs had been severely criticised in the wake of the BSE crisis, a national Meat Hygiene Service was established, taking over the responsibilities of local authorities for inspection of these premises. Local authorities remained responsible for inspection of food hygiene elsewhere.

A new national Food Standards Agency was established in 2003, a non-ministerial department with responsibilities including oversight of the Meat Hygiene Service. A new European Food Safety Authority had been established in 2002 and the law was tightened in 2006 by the European Union.

But Professor Pennington's services were soon required again, this time in Wales.

E. coli 0157 – South Wales, 2005
A major outbreak in South Wales began in August 2005. This one also originated from contaminated meat supplied by a butcher but differed from the Wishaw outbreak in certain key respects.

What happened and why?
Contaminated meat was supplied to numerous establishments in South Wales, including schools, from the premises of a catering butcher,

William Tudor in Bridgend, who also owned the abattoir supplying the butchery.

An investigation by the local authority's environmental health team discovered that some of the meals supplied to schools had been contaminated at a vacuum-packing machine at the butcher's premises.

What happened next?
Investigation and control of the outbreak was complex, eventually involving four local authorities and 44 schools, and took some time to complete. A total of 157 cases were identified, mostly affecting schoolchildren under 11 years old. Tragically, a five-year-old boy died.

Professor Pennington was again asked to carry out an inquiry and his report was published in March 2009. The full report can be read on the Welsh Assembly's website at www.wales.gov.uk. It raises a number of interesting questions, for example about 'light touch' regulation. The local authority had frequently inspected the Tudor premises and given advice, but standards had still not been brought into compliance with food safety law. How 'light' should regulation and enforcement be?

William Tudor was prosecuted, convicted and jailed for 12 months for food safety offences.

Open farms
The *E. coli* 0157 menace is not going away. It is particularly difficult to eradicate in the environment and is carried and spread by ruminant animals such as cattle, sheep and goats. In the summer of 2009 several outbreaks, one involving over 90 children, occurred at farms open to the public where children were allowed to handle animals. The outbreaks were a reminder of the danger presented by this ubiquitous pathogen. Children under five are particularly vulnerable. Fortunately none died in the 2009 outbreaks, but some were hospitalised and a few required kidney dialysis. An inquiry is ongoing at the time of writing.

Lessons
Regulation of food safety has been tightened up considerably since the UK's Food Standards Agency and a European Food Safety Authority have been established. However, there are concerns among environmental health professionals that as pressures on environmental health departments increase and resources are directed towards other priorities, emphasis on enforcement of food safety standards may not be sufficiently maintained in future.

Modern sanitation, clean drinking water, better understanding of basic hygiene, a professional environmental health service and enforceable food standards have all contributed to the highest standards of public health ever enjoyed in this country. However, the recent outbreaks such as in Lanarkshire, South Wales and some open farms warn us that we dare not become complacent about the risks from these invisible potential killers.

Some scientists and doctors are even beginning to express concern that our young people are no longer sufficiently exposed to gain immunity from some of the more common bugs that afflict us. There are new ones emerging too.

The 2009 vaccination programme to protect vulnerable groups against swine flu has recognised the risk of a global pandemic, possibly on the scale of the influenza outbreak at the end of the Great War that killed even more people than died in the trenches. Pandemics following outbreaks of SARS and bird flu, the subjects of recent scares, have mercifully not yet swept the globe and thankfully the doom-mongers' worst predictions have yet to come to pass. But there is a real danger that governments that cry wolf too often may lead us to become too relaxed about these risks.

We need to remember our history.

Sources

Broad Street pump cholera
Johnson S. *The ghost map: a street, an epidemic and the hidden power of urban networks*. London: Penguin, 2008
Snow J. *On the mode of communication of cholera* (2nd edition). London: John Churchill, 1855
Summers J. *Broad Street pump outbreak*. UCLA Department of Epidemiology School of Public Health. www.ph.ucla.edu/epi/snow/broadstreetpump.html

Wadebridge typhus
Hoyle R. *Death on the Camel*. Gemini, 1993

Birmingham smallpox
Behbehani A M. The smallpox story: life and death of an old disease. *Microbiological Review* 1983; 47 (4): 455–509
World Health Organization. Global alert and response: smallpox. www.who.int/csr/disease/smallpox/en/index.html

E. coli

BBC News Online. Sheriff criticises E. coli butcher, 19 August 1998. http://news.bbc.co.uk/1/hi/health/154107.stm

BBC News Online. Timeline: South Wales E. coli outbreak, 20 December 2005. http://news.bbc.co.uk/1/hi/wales/4284852.stm

Pennington T H. *Report on the circumstances leading to the 1996 outbreak of infection with E. coli 0157 in Central Scotland, the implications for food safety and the lessons to be learned.* Edinburgh: HMSO Scotland, 1998. www.scotland.gov.uk/library/documents-w4/pgr-00.htm

Welsh Assembly Government. Ymchwiliad Cyhoeddus E. coli / E. coli Public Inquiry. http://cymru.gov.uk/ecoliinquiry/?lang=en

General

Centers for Disease Control and Prevention. www.cdc.gov

Chartered Institute of Environmental Health. www.cieh.org

Department of Health. www.dh.gov.uk

European Food Safety Authority. www.efsa.europa.eu

Food Standards Agency. www.food.gov.uk

Health Protection Agency. www.hpa.org.uk

Chapter 28: Animal health catastrophes

Several large-scale animal disease outbreaks in the UK since the Second World War have seriously damaged the economy and had long-lasting social effects on the farming communities in which they occurred. The suffering of diseased animals and the public outrage caused by mass slaughtering of healthy stock when necessary to prevent the spread of disease are invariably highly charged political issues.

The animal health problems of the last 30 years have some interesting lessons to show us for the prevention of human health and safety disasters. Animals, just like us, are susceptible to numerous unpleasant diseases. While these cannot always be prevented – vaccination can sometimes help and high standards of biosecurity at farms are essential – an outbreak of the most virulent diseases, such as classical swine fever, foot and mouth disease or avian influenza, has to be swiftly and effectively controlled if it is not to spread widely. Some animal diseases – zoonoses – can be transferred to us.

The regulation of animal health and welfare
There is a long history to the development of controls for animal health and welfare in Britain. Like the regulation of occupational safety, health and welfare, it began to be regulated in the 19th century. But strangely the two regimes have been allowed to develop along quite separate, parallel paths, with no read-across and no communication between the professionals involved, when there could be so much to learn from each other.

An 'Act to prevent the cruel and improper Treatment of Cattle' was introduced in 1822 but local involvement in enforcement of animal health and welfare law had begun at least as early as 1798 with the Diseased Sheep Act, which involved JPs in enforcement.

The role of the state in promoting animal health became more prominent after an outbreak of sheep pox prompted Parliament to pass legislation in 1847 to prevent the introduction and spread of contagious or infectious disease among sheep, cattle and other animals. In 1865 an embryonic State Veterinary Service was formed; this was a timely move, as an outbreak of cattle plague (or rinderpest) in 1867 involved the government in a (now all too familiar) scenario of taking veterinary advice, slaughtering infected animals and restricting movements.

That same year, the Contagious Diseases (Animals) Act was introduced with the aims of promoting animal health and preventing disease, and safeguarding animals in transit. Further legislation followed in 1878, 1893, 1894 and 1910, while welfare law was consolidated in the Protection of Animals Act 1911.

In the absence of a national inspectorate for the enforcement of these controls (for the State Veterinary Service had not been conceived as such), local authorities gradually became involved in enforcing animal health and welfare laws.

The UK's entry into the European Common Market in the 1970s meant that new controls were increasingly driven by the EU system of Directives and Regulations, replacing or overlaying domestic law. After the BSE crisis, the European Commission banned the export of British beef because of concerns over the risk to human health of contracting Creutzfeldt-Jakob Disease. The consequences for the British beef industry were devastating. It would be 10 years before the ban was lifted and exports could resume.

The point of this brief historical sketch is to emphasise that there is today a very significant and complex body of law which continues to develop in this area of government. The system of controls and institutional arrangements for their delivery are deep-rooted and have been developed over a long period of time, often in response to public demands or in the light of new scientific, medical and veterinary understanding, punctuated by crises which can have the most severe consequences, including threats to human health.

Clearly, proper compliance with these controls by farmers and the food supply chain and effective enforcement by the authorities are vitally important, socially, economically and politically. Some major disasters have occurred.

The BSE disaster, UK, 1980s–1990s

One of the worst animal health disasters of the 20th century happened in the UK. It is a story of poor industrial practice, ineffective regulation, failure to apply the 'precautionary principle' in a timely fashion and weak enforcement, all leading to social and economic damage on an unprecedented scale, with thousands of animals slaughtered and an export ban imposed on British beef. Worse still, it led to the deaths of uninformed, innocent people – and there may be more to come.

What happened?

The troubling story of BSE (bovine spongiform encephalopathy) began just before Christmas 1984, when a vet was called to a Sussex farm to examine a cow suffering from loss of weight and a strangely arched back. Soon it developed head tremors and lost co-ordination, and within a few weeks it had died.

Why?
Seven months passed before the government's Central Veterinary Laboratory diagnosed the cow's illness as spongiform encephalopathy. It was still not clear what had caused this. By then, other cows were exhibiting symptoms. There were suspicions, but it would be several years before the real cause was confirmed.

What happened next?
By June 1987 four herds were affected and the Ministry of Agriculture, Fisheries and Food (MAFF) had been alerted to the disease. It was almost a year before Professor Richard Southwood of Oxford University was appointed to head a working group to investigate BSE and advise the government whether there were any implications for human health. But already suspecting that the practice that had grown up in the agricultural industry of feeding animal protein from cattle and sheep to beef cattle might be the cause, the government banned the practice outright, pending the Southwood committee's report.

Sheep had long been known to suffer quite commonly from a similar disease, scrapie, but it had never been shown to harm human beings who ate infected mutton or lamb. The Southwood Report was received in February 1989, recommending a ban on including bovine offal in baby foods. Still doubting whether BSE could be transferred from animals to humans on the basis that scrapie in sheep did not 'pass the species barrier', the committee nevertheless pointed out that if it could, the consequences for human health would be very serious.

An alarmed government decided to ban specified bovine offal (SBO) from food for human consumption. The spinal cord of cattle was to be removed in abattoirs before beef was allowed into the human food chain and all living animals showing symptoms were to be slaughtered. Farmers were compensated, but until 1990 this was only up to 50 per cent of the value of each animal.

Lessons
There was a long delay between first suspicions and effective action. In 1990 scientists had begun to think that BSE, a prion disease, could pass the species barrier when a cat became infected. Laboratory experiments then demonstrated that mice could also be infected by BSE prions. Nevertheless, the government, not wishing to cause alarm, continued to assure the public

that eating beef was safe, with a MAFF minister even seen feeding a hamburger to his daughter. A Spongiform Encephalopathy Advisory Committee (SEAC) was established to keep an eye on the situation.

BSE cases in cattle were highest between 1992 and 1993, affecting three animals in every 1000, and then declined. But by 1995 new cases of the very rare human disease CJD began to be identified, with post-mortems revealing unusual spongiform symptoms in victims' brains. This new form of the disease was named 'variant' CJD (vCJD). By 1996, eight cases of vCJD in young people had been diagnosed.

Worse was to follow: MAFF informed SEAC that during inspections of abattoirs it had discovered poor compliance with the SBO ban and removal of spinal cords. It was possible that BSE-infected material could have been entering the human food chain since 1990.

This was very bad news. SEAC advised the government in March 1996 that it was likely that the human vCJD cases were caused by eating beef contaminated with the BSE infection. Parliament was informed and the European Commission banned the export of British beef within the European Union, a ban that was to last 10 years. Another cull was ordered by the government, this time of cattle reared alongside cattle suffering with BSE between 1989 and 1993, as it was believed that these were the ones most likely to have become infected.

By now enormous economic damage had been done. The BSE crisis is estimated to have cost the British taxpayer £8 billion – roughly the cost of building the Channel Tunnel. What this does not reflect is the severity of the impact on farmers and the rural economy in spite of financial compensation – herds had to be slaughtered that had been carefully bred over generations – and the suffering of vCJD victims and their families.

It was feared that thousands of cases of vCJD would soon begin to emerge. However, this has not happened – yet. By August 2009, 164 cases had been confirmed. Some people think this is still a ticking time bomb.

This disaster was not simply caused by feeding infected animal protein to similar animals, unsavoury though that practice was. There were underlying factors leading to this disaster, as is so often the case. A close, perhaps too close, relationship existed between MAFF, the sponsoring government department, and the industry.

Weak regulation allows poor practices to take root. Who condoned the feeding of animal protein to animals in the UK, when this practice was frowned on abroad? A half-hearted attempt to raise standards was then undermined by weak enforcement in the face of poor compliance. Recognition of the risks to human health was too slow and an insufficiently precautionary approach was then taken towards preventing exposure.

Finally crowned by the European export ban, the disaster was a huge blow to the reputation of the British beef industry. The political response was to form a new agency, the Meat Hygiene Service, which took over the supervision of abattoirs from local authorities. Later, the independent Food Standards Agency would be formed, taking over the Meat Hygiene Service from MAFF.

Such an appalling animal health and human health disaster should never be allowed to happen again. But the travails of the British livestock industry were not yet over.

Foot and mouth disease, UK, 2001

The UK had not suffered a serious outbreak of foot and mouth disease (FMD) since 1967. That had not spread very widely because in those days there were many local markets and slaughterhouses and animals did not need to be taken very far.

By 2001 this had all changed considerably. Tighter European laws had led to the closure of many smaller slaughterhouses and there were fewer markets, so animals were being moved considerable distances. The risk of any infectious disease spreading far and wide was now much greater, though this had not yet been taken on board by the industry or its regulators.

What happened?

A vet working in an Essex slaughterhouse was the first to spot FMD in a batch of pigs that had been brought down from a farm in Northumbria. To the horror of the British livestock industry and the regulatory authorities, it soon became apparent from daily reports that the disease was occurring in several different parts of the country. A major outbreak was getting under way.

Why?

The FMD virus that caused the 2001 outbreak was probably imported into the UK in infected meat. Pigs on a farm near Hexham had been fed infected swill made from waste food collected from takeaways and restaurants in the North East.

Thousands of animal carcasses were burnt on pyres and buried in pits in an ultimately successful but costly attempt to rid the UK of foot and mouth disease in 2001.
Getty Images

Before the outbreak, there had been inspections of the farm by the authorities but these failed to raise its woefully poor standards. The animal welfare conditions they had observed at the farm were unacceptable. Tougher enforcement might have led to better management of the animals by the farmer and early identification of disease before it took hold and left the farm. We shall never know.

What happened next?
The ease and speed with which the disease spread after its identification in Essex were not expected and found the authorities and emergency services ill prepared. It was not immediately clear where it had originated. Desperate measures were now necessary to stamp the disease out quickly and the difficult political decision was taken to slaughter animals on farms in zones adjoining infected herds. There was no vaccination programme.

It rapidly became apparent that containment was impossible. The outbreak was spiralling out of control, more and more infected animals were being identified and this had now become a national disaster. The Prime Minister himself took charge, using his Chief Scientific Adviser to overrule officials in MAFF in whom he had no confidence.

An unwitting general public woke up to hear that the Army had been drafted in to help. They would be shocked and horrified daily by the appalling televised images of hellish funeral pyres burning the carcasses of slaughtered beasts. Outrage and anger grew as the disease ran its course and the wholesale slaughter continued.

Lessons

Quite apart from the failure of veterinary officials to remedy the disgraceful conditions at the Northumbrian farm, the now commonplace movement of animals over long distances had not been taken into account in the planning of emergency measures to restrict the spread of disease. Few of the animal health professionals who had experience of controlling the 1967 outbreak were still practising, so knowledge of what to do was limited. In any case, any lessons that had been learnt from the previous outbreak did not include the introduction of effective systems of animal identification and traceability.

The foot and mouth outbreak of 2001 is believed to have cost some £3 billion to the public sector, £5 billion to the private sector, and the lives of 6 million animals (source: National Audit Office report). The outbreak had huge social consequences for life in rural communities still recovering from the BSE disaster and for whom financial compensation for their dead animals was no compensation at all.

The damage was not to end there. The political fallout had been amplified by daily reports of the disaster on television and in the tabloids. With memories of the BSE crisis still fresh, the handling of this latest disaster by the authorities was severely criticised. It spelt the end of MAFF.

However, some good was to come out of all this. Sir Iain Anderson was asked by the government to conduct an inquiry into the outbreak and he made a number of recommendations that were implemented.

A new government department, the Department of Environment, Food and Rural Affairs (DEFRA) was to rise from the ashes of MAFF and, in close collaboration with a chastened industry, had soon introduced much tighter controls over animal movements, identification and traceability. A national emergency response plan was developed and regularly exercised. Next time, would the industry and the authorities be better prepared?

Foot and mouth disease, Pirbright, England, 2007

Ironically, the source of the next UK outbreak of foot and mouth disease was to be a site shared by a private firm, Merial, and a DEFRA government laboratory researching animal diseases and developing vaccines. But thanks to the lessons learned from the 2001 outbreak, this one was swiftly contained.

What happened?

Eight cases of FMD occurred during August and September 2007 in a relatively small area of south-east England.

Why?
Live foot and mouth virus, stored and used in DEFRA's Institute of
Animal Health laboratory at Pirbright, Surrey, under what should have
been very tight containment for research purposes, was escaping into a
drainage system long overdue for repair. Contaminated effluent leaking
from broken drains was then being carried unknowingly from the site,
probably by vehicles or pedestrians, onto the road and then a track
leading to a nearby farm, where animals began to sicken. The Pirbright
laboratory was self-regulated and the risk presented by the neglect of the
drains had not been picked up by officials.

What happened next?
Foot and mouth disease was swiftly identified by vets. Animal movements
were immediately restricted, effectively preventing the further spread of
the disease. Sick animals were slaughtered and others vaccinated, while the
export of animals susceptible to FMD was suspended.

That FMD should have revisited the UK so soon after 2001 – and
particularly around Pirbright, believed to be a centre of excellence for
animal health research – set everyone in a spin. A welter of reviews was
urgently set in motion.

An epidemiological investigation was launched to determine when
infection was introduced and all possible sources of infection. It involved
investigating possible movements of susceptible animals and their
products, people, vehicles, equipment, feedstuffs, bedding material, and a
possible link to the activities being undertaken at the Pirbright research
site.

By the end of August, this investigation had concluded that release of live
FMD virus was most likely to have occurred as a result of the escape of
the virus from the drainage system that connected the vaccine production
plant to the sodium hydroxide treatment tanks on another part of the
Pirbright laboratory site. Movement of the virus off site was most likely
from movement of 'fomites' (substances capable of carrying infectious
organisms) created from soil, water or other material that had been
contaminated by effluent, and then deposited on the road from which the
track to the first infected premises led.

The HSE was asked to carry out an investigation of the Pirbright site. The
HSE had been inspecting other sites handling dangerous pathogens, such
as Porton Down, for many years and possessed an experienced cadre of
inspectors with the necessary scientific, technical and medical expertise.

They soon confirmed poor risk management and inadequate maintenance of the drains as the cause of the escape of the live FMD virus and recommended a review of the regulatory framework for animal pathogens.

Lessons

Sir Bill Callaghan, a former chairman of the Health and Safety Commission, was asked to carry out the regulatory review. It was not surprising that a key recommendation was for the HSE to take over responsibility for regulation and inspection of the Pirbright site from DEFRA, so enabling disinterested supervision by an independent regulator.

Sir Iain Anderson, who had led the inquiry into the 2001 FMD disaster, was asked to review the government's reaction to the 2007 outbreak, to review the lessons he had drawn from the 2001 outbreak, and to identify any others arising from the latest one.

Yet another independent review of issues raised by the investigations was commissioned by DEFRA and carried out by Professor Brian Spratt of Imperial College London University, who reported to the Secretary of State and the Chief Veterinary Officer with a number of suggestions to improve biosecurity and biosafety, both at the Pirbright site and to ensure the future safety of all laboratories that work on FMD virus and other exotic animal pathogens.

By December 2007 it was possible to lift all movement restrictions and resume trade within the EU, no more cases of FMD having occurred. The United Kingdom's official report on the outbreak was submitted to the OIE (World Organisation for Animal Health) and in February 2008 the OIE confirmed that the UK was once again 'a foot and mouth disease-free country without vaccination'.

Meanwhile the HSE and DEFRA had committed themselves to a joint programme of inspections to ensure that every issue raised by these investigations was properly reviewed. The inspections covered all laboratory and manufacturing facilities in Great Britain that were working with hazardous biological agents at 'containment levels 3 and 4' to which the Control of Substances Hazardous to Health Regulations 2002 and the Genetically Modified Organisms (Contained Use) Regulations 2000 applied, or with 'group 4' specified animal pathogens covered by the Specified Animal Pathogens Order 1998.

The first phase concentrated on the higher risk 'CL 4' facilities. No breaches of law were discovered and no formal enforcement action was needed. A second phase to 'CL 3' facilities was completed in 2008. This programme of inspections enabled advice and guidance on good practice to be shared between the regulatory bodies and the laboratory operators and provided both parties with assurance that the facilities were being well managed.

So where does this leave animal health in the UK today? This time catastrophe had been averted, but have the lessons of the past been learned sufficiently to prevent future disasters? Yet again the weakness of self-regulation had been exposed. The need for oversight of an industry not by a sponsoring government department but by an independent, disinterested regulator had, yet again, to be recognised.

There are some encouraging signs for the future. As well as tightening controls over animal health, the UK government has ratified the European Conventions relating to the transport of animals and keeping of animals for farming and scientific purposes. And animal welfare standards are steadily being raised in response to strong public opinion: the recent Animal Welfare Act has been hailed on the DEFRA website as "the most significant animal welfare legislation for nearly a century".

Sources

BSE
Lord Phillips of Worth Matravers. *The BSE Inquiry: the report*. London: HMSO, 2000.
Packer R. *The politics of BSE*. London: Palgrave Macmillan, 2006

Foot and mouth 2001
Anderson I. *Foot and mouth disease: lessons to be learned. Inquiry report* (HC888). London: The Stationery Office, 2002. http://archive.cabinetoffice.gov.uk/fmd/fmd_report/report/index.htm
BBC News Online – in depth. Foot-and-mouth outbreak, 23 January 2003. http://news.bbc.co.uk/1/hi/in_depth/uk/2001/foot_and_mouth/default.stm

Foot and mouth 2007
BBC News Online. Foot-and-mouth 'traced to pipe', 5 September 2007. http://news.bbc.co.uk/1/hi/uk/6979891.stm
Cabinet Office. Foot and mouth review 2007. http://archive.cabinetoffice.gov.uk/fmdreview (includes links to Sir Iain Anderson's reports and government responses)
Health and Safety Executive. Investigation of foot and mouth outbreak. www.hse.gov.uk/news/archive/07aug/footandmouth.htm (includes links to draft and final reports)

Chapter 29: Bhopal

"The gas moved like a phantom."
(The Council of Scientific and Industrial Research, India)

I have saved the worst disaster until the end.

The lethally toxic gas released at Bhopal, India, in the world's most dreadful chemical industry disaster is believed to have killed over 5,000 people and harmed another 200,000 (source: *The Sunday Times*, From the Archive 5 July 2009). Other sources suggest far more. These estimates will never be confirmed, as over the years many people have continued to die from exposure to the gas. Over half a million people have since received compensation from a settlement of $470 million made by Union Carbide, the company that owned and operated the plant. To this day the site remains severely contaminated.

What happened?
Union Carbide India Ltd's plant at Bhopal manufactured pesticides, using methyl isocyanate (known as 'MIC'), a highly toxic substance, as an intermediate in the manufacture of carbaryl. During the night shift on 2 December 1984 at around 11 pm, the temperature and pressure began to rise in a storage tank containing 3,840 gallons of liquid MIC. Spotted by operators, there was an attempt to control this runaway reaction by using hosepipes to direct cooling water onto the tank. The attempt failed and just after midnight a relief valve lifted, releasing deadly gas. A rumbling sound is said to have been heard by operators and a screeching noise as the gas began to vent.

Operators tried to switch on the plant's vent gas scrubber but this was found to be inoperable. No effective warning could be sounded as the main alarm system was out of action. For several hours the tank continued to vent its contents. The lethal gas, heavier than air, rolled silently out of the plant into the surrounding housing where thousands of people were asleep with their windows open. Many of them were to perish within minutes of exposure.

As hours passed, the gas cloud continued to drift onwards into central Bhopal, eventually covering an area of some 25 square miles. It would be nearly two o'clock in the morning before outside help arrived. By now thousands of people and animals had been affected, many choking or blinded or killed by exposure to the gas. Many others would die in the years to come.

Victims of the MIC
leak at Bhopal the
day after, December
1984.
pulzinponderland.
wordpress.com

The resources of the emergency services and hospital staff were completely overwhelmed.

Why?

The technical cause is believed to lie in the temperature of the MIC in the storage tank rising because of contamination of the process liquid by water. It is not known with certainty why or how the water came to be present in this tank, though it is thought to have been due to failure of blind connecting pipework during maintenance of an adjacent storage tank. The presence of water in the process fluid caused an exothermic reaction, and as the temperature rose, so did the pressure, gasifying the liquid MIC until the relief valve lifted and released the gas to the atmosphere.

The root causes are more complex. Among Bhopal's population of 670,000, about 12,000 people lived in the immediate vicinity of the plant. Arguably, the plant should never have been located so close to a major town, but this is by no means the only example of a shanty town being allowed to spring up around the perimeter fence of a facility in the absence of any planning restrictions.

No thought had been given to the potential effects on this population of an accident at the plant, no proper emergency procedures were in place, and on the night of the disaster any safety systems that might have contained the release of gas were inoperable, and had been for some time.

A refrigeration system that might have kept the tank's temperature down had been decommissioned. A flare tower and vent gas scrubber system critical to safe working of the plant had been inoperable for several months before the incident.

The local population was unaware of any alarm systems that might have alerted them. Indeed, the plant's main audible warning system was inoperable. Although a secondary siren was available to operators, they were unsure whether to use it in case it caused panic. When they did, the siren failed to awaken many of the people sleeping nearby, let alone in central Bhopal.

The failure to develop an emergency plan that considered the risks to the general public meant that no adequate response had been planned by the authorities. The resources of the emergency services were overwhelmed by the magnitude of this unforeseen but foreseeable disaster. Attempts by medical staff to help victims were hampered by lack of information about the effects of exposure to MIC.

What happened next?
The plant operator, Union Carbide, was blamed by the Indian government and accused of cost-cutting and neglect of safety measures. The company argued in its defence that safety measures were adequate but the plant had been sabotaged.

The chairman of Union Carbide flew to India only to find himself placed under arrest. Released on bail, he left the country, never to return. A warrant for his arrest in India for manslaughter remains outstanding.

The company eventually settled claims for compensation for the sum of $470 million out of court. However, legal wrangling about the inadequacy of this sum continued for years afterwards: $15 billion had originally been claimed.

Lessons
The lessons to be learnt from this shameful episode, according to the HSE website advice on major accident hazards, are as follows:

The flare system was a critical element within the plant's protection system. However, this fact was not recognised as it was out of commission for some three months prior to the accident.

Hazards associated with runaway reactions in a chemical reactor are generally understood. However, such an occurrence within a storage tank had received little research.

The rusting remains of the Union Carbide factory in Bhopal, around 20 years later.
Luca Frediani

The ingress of water caused an exothermic reaction with the process fluid. The exact point of ingress is uncertain though poor modification/ maintenance practices may have contributed.

Decommissioning of the refrigeration system was one plant modification that contributed to the accident. Without this system the temperature within the tank was higher than the design temperature of 0 °C.

The emergency response from the company to the incident and from the local authority suggests that the emergency plan was ineffective. During the emergency operators hesitated when to use the siren system. No information was available regarding the hazardous nature of MIC and what medical actions should be taken.

Clearly, there was no culture of safety worth speaking of at the plant. The people who had been allowed to erect and live in the ramshackle dwellings which clustered around the factory fence were at great risk if anything went seriously wrong. It should never have been allowed and the local planning authority should have had some questions to answer.

Building houses so close to any major hazard plant is highly undesirable. But did we learn? See Buncefield...

Sources

Apex Press. Bhopal Library (collection of material on the disaster). www.cipa-apex.org/books/bhopal

BBC News Online. Bhopal's health effects probed, 26 March 2009. http://news.bbc.co.uk/1/hi/sci/tech/7961062.stm

Union Carbide Corporation. Bhopal information center. www.bhopal.com

Chapter 30: Reducing hazards and risks

"Our main objective was to keep the air in and the water out."
(The late Sir John Harvey-Jones, former Chairman of ICI, talking about his experience as a submariner in the Second World War)

Amid the tragedies and catastrophes described in the foregoing chapters, there is at least one positive outcome. Over the past century, legislators have learnt lessons that have helped them shape the law and create an environment in which businesses and people can choose to prosper in safety. Indeed, it is usually politically impossible to ratchet up standards unless there has been a disaster pointing the way forward, setting a mood among the general public that something must be done.

This was true in the period after the Second World War as Britain's economy slowly recovered and grew. Public expectations of a better society led to growing disquiet about the mounting toll of deaths and serious injuries at work, leading to the establishment of an inquiry to look into the state of health and safety at work in Great Britain – the Robens Committee, chaired by Lord Robens, head of the National Coal Board. No doubt his own thinking had been shaped by the dreadful experience of the tragedy at Aberfan (see Chapter 1). The new law that resulted from that inquiry set goals to be achieved by employers based on the duty of care in common law. So far as was reasonably practicable, they were to ensure the health and safety of their workers and make sure that the way they conducted their enterprise did not endanger the general public. These principles were enshrined in the general duties of the Health and Safety at Work etc Act 1974 and continue to apply today. Essentially, they are about reducing hazards and risks.

The starting point for avoiding disaster is to recognise the hazards you have around you and then do whatever is reasonably practicable to reduce them. For example, in one case it may be enough to prevent contact with dangerous parts of machinery. In another, say where a population is at risk from flooding, it may be necessary to go to the trouble of installing elaborate and expensive flood protection measures, such as the Thames Barrier. What is judged reasonably practicable to reduce a risk will depend on the time, cost and trouble weighed against the size of the risk each hazard presents.

Hazard and risk are often confused. Much has been said and written in recent years about risk assessment, but if you haven't recognised a hazard you can't assess the potential risk. An example is the *E. coli* 0157 bacterium, a potentially lethal hazard which many people do not understand. As we have seen earlier, the strictest hygiene precautions are needed in food preparation to control the risk from the *E. coli* hazard and prevent the harm it may do to consumers.

Risk is simply the chance of a hazard doing harm to someone or the environment. So if you can eliminate the hazard entirely, you won't face that risk and won't need to assess it. If you can't do that but can still reduce the hazard, then the risk will be reduced as well.

Where a hazard can be avoided by being safely 'designed out' of a process, it will always be the best starting point. After Flixborough, a great deal of effort was put in by members of the chemical engineering profession to pursuing the benefits of 'inherently safer design', led by Trevor Kletz. For example, eliminating a toxic substance from a process by substituting a less harmful chemical that is equally effective would always be good. In the 1960s, persuading printers to stop using benzene for cleaning ink from the rollers of printing presses and instead use the safer solvents that had become available probably prevented many cases of cancer in that industry.

We have been less successful with asbestos and have the legacy of many years of usage still to manage, but here an example would be to leave well-protected asbestos insulation alone and undisturbed, properly identified and logged. In the event of any work being necessary that might disturb it, this will enable the hazard to be recognised and properly communicated to any workers involved. Any harm to them can then be prevented by making sure that they are well protected and taking appropriate precautions, whether it be during the simple drilling of a wall with a portable tool or the total demolition of a building.

It is not always feasible to eliminate a hazard, but often it can be reduced. We have seen in earlier chapters that regulatory authorities became concerned about the increasing sizes of inventories of hazardous materials stored on sites and the severe consequences for people and the environment when things go wrong. Reducing inventories, process temperatures and pressures where possible can reduce the hazard considerably. Following this advice before some of the major incidents described in these pages might have reduced the severity of the consequences of a fire or explosion. As Trevor Kletz has said, "If you don't need it, don't keep it."

Risk assessment is simply the step between identifying a hazard and controlling the risk; it is an essential means to the end but never the end itself, which is about adopting the right control measures.

Choosing the right precautions is the final key to success. There will be a spectrum of options to be taken, ranging from elimination, substitution or engineering controls to personal protective equipment or a combination of these.

We have also seen that the human factor must never be forgotten. Humankind's capacity for mastering technology is remarkable but the way people are likely to behave when faced with the unexpected needs to be taken fully into account when designing systems of work or introducing technological changes and in training and supervising staff. Where confusion reigns, chaos follows. Some of the disasters I have described, such as Three Mile Island and Chernobyl, are extreme examples. When people are put under pressure they can make serious mistakes of judgment, as the *Challenger* disaster illustrates, or in ignorance of danger some may run unnecessary risks for the sake of reward, as in the Morecambe Bay tragedy, or simply to try and do well.

Good communication about hazard and risk is vital. It is no use having an expensive consultant produce an elaborate risk assessment for you if managers do not communicate its findings properly. The workforce will not understand it and will not accept that they need to follow procedures and take certain precautions.

As so many of the examples in the preceding chapters show, it is astonishing how often organisations can get it badly wrong.

The HSE has provided valuable guidance on how to get it right. Its *Five steps to risk assessment* was intended to provide information to small firms in low-risk sectors but its essential logic is applicable to all. Identifying the hazard may require only a visual inspection in a simple case, but where processes are more complex it will need a more systematic approach such as a HAZOP (Hazard and Operability) study. The population exposed to the hazard, whether workers or the general public, must of course be taken into account. Deciding how the hazard may be eliminated or reduced, and then deciding when this has been done how any remaining risk should be kept as low as reasonably practicable leads to vital decisions about control measures.

The Aberfan disaster (Chapter 1) is a tragic example of how none of this was done, but the legal requirements for the stability of tips that were subsequently introduced are an example of how the risk assessment process can help avoid another tragedy. Arrangements have to be made to consider tips' foundations and the nature of the geological strata beneath them, natural features such as springs and streams, the kind of spoil being tipped, and so on. The owner or manager has to specify the manner of tipping, tip supervision, the nature and frequency of the appointed surveyor's inspections, and any action to be taken if these reveal a defect. Regular safety audits of active and closed tips must be carried out by an independent competent person. Weekly inspections are required of active tips. This is all no more than good practice now enshrined in law, and by being followed it has succeeded in preventing another Aberfan.

Sources

Health and Safety Executive. *Five steps to risk assessment* (INDG 163(rev2)). Sudbury: HSE Books, 2006. www.hse.gov.uk/pubns/indg163.pdf

Health and Safety Executive. *Reducing risks, protecting people.* Sudbury: HSE Books, 2001. www.hse.gov.uk/risk/theory/r2p2.pdf

Health and Safety Executive. *Successful health and safety management* (HSG65). Sudbury: HSE Books, 1999. www.hse.gov.uk/pubns/priced/hsg65.pdf

Health and Safety Executive. *The tolerability of risk from nuclear power stations.* London: HMSO, 1988. www.hse.gov.uk/nuclear/tolerability.pdf

IOSH. *Learning the lessons: how to respond to deaths at work and other serious incidents.* Wigston: IOSH, 2008. www.iosh.co.uk/information_and_resources/guidance_and_tools.aspx

Chapter 31: The politics of disaster

Politics are inescapable. As we have seen in earlier chapters, most disasters are accompanied by demands for retribution and that something should be done to prevent a recurrence, usually evoking the response that 'lessons will be learned'. Governments and their ministers have usually wished to be seen to be reacting quickly to public outrage and showing sensitivity to the wishes of victims and their families. They will often do this by using statutory powers to initiate an independent investigation, appointing an eminent QC or respected expert to lead it.

Some may regard this as a cynical move designed to kick the issue into the long grass, but there is no doubting that over the years the recommendations of inquiries have usually resulted in change for the better, even if some lessons are soon forgotten.

Witnesses give their evidence and are cross-examined in public, followed by the publication of a report with findings and recommendations. The government of the day will normally respond by adopting the recommendations in the form of a change in the law or reorganisation or invention of new regulatory institutions. For example, the poor safety performance of the 1960s led to the recommendations of the Robens Committee, the Health and Safety at Work etc Act 1974 and a new national health and safety regulator. At the European level, after a series of human and environmental disasters, the Seveso Directives were enacted to cover risks from major hazard installations.

Public inquiries

We have seen that some inquiries have taken place and reported very quickly, for example after Aberfan (1966) in 1967 and Flixborough (1974) in 1975. These days, public inquiries are becoming increasingly expensive, slow and adversarial, possibly because of the development of a 'compensation culture' and a more litigious society.

The parties to the inquiry will now normally be represented by counsel who will want – and are usually permitted – to examine witnesses at length, bearing in mind the possibility of civil actions for compensation of victims and the potential liabilities of their clients.

The costs of some recent inquiries have run into many millions of pounds, a prime example being the Saville inquiry into Bloody Sunday, still ongoing 11 years after starting. This was set up in 1998 by Tony Blair, then Prime Minister, as the second public inquiry into the tragic event in

Northern Ireland on 30 January 1972. The first inquiry by Lord Widgery had reported within 11 weeks and was regarded as a whitewash, leaving everyone dissatisfied.

Governments may therefore be reluctant to go down the public inquiry path if another equally effective and swifter means of bringing the facts to light and learning lessons can be found. The commissioning of the investigation and report by the HSE into the 1984 Abbeystead disaster was such an example, where the regulator's findings were accepted and there was no demand subsequently for a public inquiry. On the other hand, in spite of public demands, the sinking of the *Marchioness* in 1989 was not subject to an independent public inquiry until a new government (which, while in opposition, had promised to hold one) was elected in 1997. Even then, the inquiry did not take place until three years later.

One has to wonder whether the facts can really be established accurately after such a passage of time. But in some cases it proves politically impossible to resist public demands for an independent inquiry. A new factor, today, will be where a regulatory authority is thought possibly to have shared responsibility for failing to prevent a disaster and is 'in the dock' together with the owner or operator of the premises or plant. The regulator's own internal inquiry into its actions, even where the investigation includes an independent outsider and its report is subsequently published, may not be seen to be sufficiently impartial. The Ladbroke Grove rail disaster and more recently the ICL explosion in Glasgow are examples where politicians, sensitive to public perceptions, have insisted on an inquiry that is seen to be independent of the safety regulator.

Prosecutions, where the evidence is available and they are judged to be in the public interest, may also be long delayed. The cases against the operators of the Buncefield site are coming to court in 2010, nearly five years after the disastrous explosion; the cases against the parties arraigned in France after the Concorde crash in 2000 seem likely to be heard at least 10 years after the event.

Justice delayed is justice denied.

Corporate killing

After a disaster occurs there is no escaping the natural and understandable desire of victims and their families for justice, the public's anger and the demands for retribution fanned by lurid headlines in the tabloid press, like 'Heads should roll!' or 'Someone must pay!' Public outrage following the failure of prosecutions of companies for corporate manslaughter under the existing law, such as followed the *Herald of Free Enterprise* disaster in 1987, led to a vigorous and persistent campaign by victims' groups and trade unions for a change in the law to secure convictions and heavy penalties for 'corporate killing'.

Nearly a decade passed before Parliament enacted a change. In 2001 the Home Office began consultations on proposals that a company should be guilty of corporate killing if a management failure by the corporation were the cause, or one of the causes, of a person's death and if that failure constituted conduct falling far below what could reasonably be expected in the circumstances. The penalty in such a case would be an unlimited fine.

Individuals within a company would still be liable for the offences of reckless killing and killing by gross carelessness. The prosecution of individual directors and managers under Section 37 of the 1974 Act would also remain an option.

The proposals were controversial and were naturally strongly opposed by employers' representatives. But given the background of several recent major catastrophes resulting in multiple deaths and public outrage, it was really only a matter of time before the offence of corporate killing would reach the statute book. The government had promised action to change the law several times and the Prime Minister reaffirmed its intentions at the TUC's conference in 2004.

After much further consultation and dithering by ministers over issues such as Crown immunity and deaths in custody, a bill was finally passed by Parliament, the Corporate Manslaughter and Corporate Homicide Act 2007 (CMCHA). It came into effect on 6 April 2008.

The new offence

It is important to note that the new Act did not create any new duties; these were already contained in the civil law of negligence. The Act created a new offence based on those existing common law duties.

In England and Wales and in Northern Ireland the offence is 'corporate manslaughter' whereas in Scotland it is known as 'corporate homicide'. A public or private 'organisation' (including partnerships, trade unions and employers' associations) may now be convicted of corporate manslaughter or homicide if the way in which its activities are 'managed' or 'organised' causes a person's death and amounts to a 'gross breach' of a 'duty of care' towards the deceased person.

The elements of this offence merit closer examination. A substantial part of the failure within the organisation must exist at a 'senior level'. 'Senior level' means the people who make significant decisions about the organisation or substantial parts of it and includes people in centralised headquarters functions as well as in operational management roles.

A 'gross breach' is one in which the organisation's conduct has fallen far below what could have been reasonably expected. In considering this, juries are expected to take account of the seriousness of any breaches of health and safety law that may have occurred, how the activity causing the death was managed or organised within the organisation, whether there were any systems and processes for managing safety, and how these were operated in practice.

Whether the 'duty of care' owed to people has been met by an organisation could thus depend on any one of several factors – for example, a system of work, equipment provided for the use of employees, the condition of premises and sites occupied by the organisation or the products or services it has supplied.

Thus, in a nutshell, companies and organisations can now be found guilty of corporate manslaughter as a result of serious management failures resulting in a gross breach of a duty of care. The Act also largely removed the Crown immunity that applied to the previous common law corporate manslaughter offence, though there are some exemptions covering public policy decisions and the exercise of public functions.

If convicted, an organisation will be subject to an unlimited fine. The courts may also impose a 'publicity order', requiring the organisation to publicise details of its conviction and fine, in effect 'naming and shaming' itself. Even so, the new Act falls short of what some campaigners had desired: company directors will not be jailed for the new offence. Prosecutions under the new Act will be of the corporate body, not of individuals.

But directors, board members and other individuals continue to be liable under health and safety law (Section 37 of the Health and Safety at Work etc Act 1974) under which the courts may impose unlimited fines or custodial sentences. Over the years a number of directors and managers convicted of serious health and safety offences have found themselves in jail.

And corporate bodies may still be prosecuted for health and safety offences as well as for corporate manslaughter.

So has anything really been gained after all those years of argument? It remains to be seen whether the authorities have an appetite for prosecuting under the new Act, and whether it will meet the expectations of the campaigning groups. Mounting these cases – and defending them – promises to be very costly.

Deaths at work must now be investigated by both the police and the relevant safety authority so that possible offences of individual or corporate manslaughter are properly considered, as well as breaches of health and safety law. The evidence will be reviewed by the Crown Prosecution Service, which, if satisfied by the evidence, will submit the case to the Director of Public Prosecutions, who will decide whether prosecution is in the public interest.

So far, only one prosecution has been launched under CMCHA following a fatal injury at work. The hearing of that case together with charges under Section 37 of the Health and Safety at Work etc Act will begin at Bristol Crown Court in February 2010.

In the meantime, trade unions continue to press their demands for the health and safety duties of directors to be redefined and enshrined in new law, with stiffer penalties and custodial sentences for offenders. Not everyone shares such a draconian view. The present government decided not to require companies to include a report of their health and safety performance in annual company reports, though many big companies choose to do this voluntarily. There are other straws in the wind.

I have mentioned 'light touch' regulation in an earlier chapter. There have been attempts in the past to deregulate and reduce burdens on business ('red tape'). In October 2009 the Conservative Party published the 'Penrose report', *Regulation in the post-bureaucratic age*, part of which said:

> A Conservative government will encourage professional standards wherever possible and appropriate, before considering Government regulations instead. We will also consider and consult on a new model of professional co-regulation. This means replacing regulator-run public teams of inspectors with a model closer to financial controls and audits. Well run companies would employ professionally qualified experts in, for example, health and safety or food safety, in the same way as they use accountants in a finance function to ensure that the correct internal processes and controls are in place, and that audited reports are reliable. An external member of the same profession would be paid to audit them in the same way as a company's financial accounts, and to issue an audit opinion that they are

satisfactory. This could be filed with the regulator (like filing annual accounts at Companies House).

It is not the first time this kind of idea has surfaced, though the vocabulary might have changed. In the early 1980s, when there was similar talk of reducing red tape and burdens on business, the Health and Safety Commission published a chapter in their Annual Report proposing 'safety assurance' – a similar form of self-regulation. It was vehemently opposed by trade unions that feared the consequences for their members and the idea foundered.

In theory, the advantages of this approach are that the regulator would have a quick and evidence-driven way to identify low-risk organisations and target their resources for inspections in more deserving directions. Regulated organisations would benefit by regaining control of the timing and method of any assessments and improvements to their internal processes and, once their audited reports were on file, would become exempt from external inspections by the regulator too. Equally, the audited reports should reduce contractual red tape and pressure from insurance companies for higher premiums.

It will only take another disaster to blow all this out of the water.

Sources

Corporate Manslaughter and Corporate Homicide Act 2007

Health and Safety at Work etc Act 1974

Ministry of Justice. www.justice.gov.uk

Penrose J. *Regulation in the post-bureaucratic age.* Conservative Party policy paper. www.epolitix.com/fileadmin/epolitix/stakeholders/BetterRegulation.pdf

Chapter 32: Establishing a culture of safety

Those who cannot remember the past are condemned to repeat it.
(George Santayana, philospher, 1863–1952)

As I hope I have shown in the foregoing chapters, it is possible to learn something from other people's mistakes and avoid disaster. A learning organisation will do better than one with a closed corporate mind. Attitudes towards risk do change in the light of experience and people take more care. But corporate memories can be very short.

There are some very simple things to remember.

As we have seen, hazard identification, their elimination or reduction, and risk assessment of the remaining hazards are the first steps to managing risks. These vital steps must be taken correctly. The even more vital step is then to adopt the appropriate controls, communicate the reasons for them to the workforce, and embed them in the company's systems of work.

Managing risks successfully over time is difficult and requires leadership and determination. It will be necessary to establish a culture of health and safety which will make it natural both for the workforce and the board and senior managers to seek risk reductions as second nature. Over time, reducing hazards and controlling risks should then become easier. A company that has a strong safety culture is usually also one that is doing well commercially.

When I have mentioned 'safety culture' in these pages, I have used the term as shorthand for a company's way of doing things that embraces the protection of safety, health and the environment. English is a wonderful language but we do not yet have a single word for all of these. The French call it *sécurité*. But whatever the language, 'safety culture' is recognisable, like an elephant. It is an attitude, detectable both in the board room and on the shop floor. It shows in company behaviour. An inspector can almost smell it.

Fashions change; much has been written about 'human factors' and more is being written today about 'behavioural safety'. These are valid attempts to grapple with the challenging interface between humans and technology. But as an inspector arriving at a works, I soon learnt to recognise the tell-tale signs of a poor safety culture. It could be seen in broken machinery left littering the yard, rusting drums of chemicals or the mysterious absence of senior managers.

A positive culture is also quickly detected from simple things, such as attitudes towards cleanliness and tidy housekeeping, lack of fear among the workforce and a willingness by both managers and workers to share a conversation about problems and solutions. A 'no-blame culture' such as exists in the aviation industry, encouraging the reporting of near misses so that everyone can learn from the experience and avoid disaster, is worth aiming at in any company. And systems such as for regular plant inspection, maintenance and permits to work will be well organised, properly documented and kept up to date. Successful management of health, safety and the environment and the avoidance of disaster is not rocket science but it does require leadership, determination, communication and a willingness to learn from any mistakes and share the lessons.

Without leadership, all this will fail, possibly with disastrous consequences. The board will need to demonstrate an unswerving commitment to the company's health, safety and environmental policies and communicate to both the company's workforce and its business partners its determination for the company to succeed in these areas. Establishing a culture of safety will protect the company. Directors will be wise to keep under review the way in which their activities are managed and organised by the company's senior management. If all goes wrong, defending a charge of manslaughter is likely to prove very expensive and damaging to corporate and individual reputations, whatever the outcome. It is far better to stay out of court – and jail.

We are talking about men and women that we know, our own people, going to work in the morning and coming home again safely to their families at night. Nothing can be more important than that.

Sources

Eves D and Gummer J. *Questioning performance: the director's essential guide to managing health, safety and the environment.* Wigston: IOSH Services Ltd, 2005
Health and Safety Executive. *Leading health and safety at work: leadership actions for directors and board members* (INDG417). Sudbury: HSE Books, 2007. www.hse.gov.uk/pubns/indg417.pdf
Health and Safety Executive. *Successful health and safety management* (HSG65). Sudbury: HSE Books, 1999. www.hse.gov.uk/pubns/priced/hsg65.pdf
IOSH. *Business risk management – getting health and safety firmly on the agenda.* Wigston: IOSH, 2006. www.iosh.co.uk/information_and_resources/guidance_and_tools.aspx
IOSH. *Promoting a positive culture – a guide to health and safety culture.* Wigston: IOSH, 2004. www.iosh.co.uk/information_and_resources/guidance_and_tools.aspx

Index